Escape from Zoomanity

VOL 1

ALAN FORREST SMITH

NEW YORK

ESCAPE FROM ZOOMANITY VOL 1

by ALAN FORREST SMITH

ISBN 978-1-61448-077-8 Paperback
ISBN 978-1-61448-078-5 eBook
ISBN 978-1-61448-079-2 Hard Cover
Library of Congress Control Number: 2011933171

Published by:
MORGAN JAMES PUBLISHING
The Entrepreneurial Publisher
5 Penn Plaza, 23rd Floor
New York City, New York 10001
(212) 655-5470 Office
(516) 908-4496 Fax
www.MorganJamesPublishing.com

Dedication

To my four amazing children: Christian, you are true genius; Elliot, you are my rock star; Ollie, you are my silent giant; and my wee darling Lily, every time we are together your wonderful, smiling spirit inspires me.

Also to my mother, thank you for your fire, thunder and crazy spirit. Dad, thank you for your gentle but loyal nature.

My brother Steve for being there for me during the dark days, I love that you are what a big brother should be.

To all of those who have affected my life in some way, for the experiences, the conversations and the moments that have given my life what is has shaped into today. You know who you are.

And of course, to my Creator.

Thank you.

Table of Contents

Table of Contents

Preface

Why Escape from Zoomanity?

At the age of 45 I was asking *what the hell is going on?*"? This is the age when almost everyone I knew had faced some kind of personal life trauma. Promises of better education, following the mainstream guidance, doing what they were told appeared to have failed them and they knew it.

People, friends, family had let them down, things they had loved, adored had gone, careers revealed themselves as a veneer not to be trusted. In reflection something was wrong with something?

My own life had also been a roller coaster at this point. My own intense spiritual experiences had locked me in and spat me out. My life had played a similar game to me. I lost everything, horrible, bitter divorce, humiliating bankruptcy, loss of my own family, disconnect from my children, the home I had built gone, even my dog Meg and my cat Yo-Yo... gone! It wasn't unique, I wasn't alone in this.

This book is a reflection of life, a reflection and feel of what appears to be an 'invisible control' feeds most of mankind what they desire, not what they need leaving people wrecked in it's Tsunami like wake!

As you pour through Escape from Zoomanity's pages you'll see yourself, you'll read yourself, you'll feel things that maybe you haven't felt for a long time, you'll just know! You'll also discover your next step.

Escape from Zoomanity has been 48 years in the making and taken me around 3 years to write, re-write and re-write again. I would probably re-write again if I had the time.

This is a message about escape, about awakening, about adventure, about a moment when you finally realize, finally awaken and then take that moment, that one decision forever to - Escape From Zoomanity.

Me, Mum & Dad

'Mum, can you make sure everything is fine at my house while I'm away please?'

'Where are you going?'

'I'm flying out to California to write a book.'

'What do you mean write a book, a book on what? How can you write a book – you're just a hairdresser!' (My mum has never got over the fact I stopped being a hairdresser in 2003.)

Biting my lip and staying as calm as I can, I reply, 'Can you just make sure my house and things are fine please mum?'

She walks away and I can hear her tell my dad that maybe I'm having another breakdown and he should speak to me. Dad mumbles then it all goes quiet.

I love my mum but she's my mum.

She's like a lot of people, a lot of mums, a lot of dads. They are born into their life. They live and experience it all, the heartache, the smiles, the pains, the loves, the experiences, the magic moments, and then of course death.

Mum and dad, like most of mankind, question almost nothing in life, and go along with almost everything that is fed to them from external sources, thoughts, behaviours, beliefs, and actions. They do as they are told and live as they are expected to live. They behave, stay in line, and play the game of Zoomanity.

It's not a bad life. It can be a great life – wealthy, healthy or whatever you need – but it's nothing extraordinary. You know, different, alive, exciting, fresh. Certainly not the way humans were created to live.

Mum and dad's life, like most of Zoomanity, is average. It's not their fault and most are happy with a life like that, with average expectations usually built around more gain – cars, homes, holidays, wages, careers. A gain that cannot guarantee or promise to bring happiness to the person whose life is built around the fear of losing what they have gained or the fear of never gaining what they have been told life is all about.

The happiness of most of mankind is continually based on a future time. 'I can't wait until…'

The problem with a future time is it never truly arrives.

Does tomorrow ever really come?

When happiness is based on the future, we live our life faster and rarely in the moment. The reason is that we are mentally trained through what we'll call *repeatism* and *conditioning* to believe and accept that we are not happy *now* but *will be* when we get what we are told we need.

In other words, it's future based.

Zoomanity is clever don't you agree?

My parents still ask me questions like –

- Why are you doing that?

- Should you be doing that?

- You can't do that, can you?

- Why are you making your life harder?

- Just accept it as it is and get on with it!

- Stop asking questions!

- Can't you just do what you're told?

Does that sounds familiar or ring true in your life? It's almost like an endless song of blind faith.

The masses of mankind live by one rule and one rule only:

Zoomanity Tells Us to Believe and Question Nothing

Do as you're told. Believe what you're told. Question nothing. Do that and they (the zoo keepers) will look after you.

That's it, the philosophy in a nutshell. If you want to be happy, do as you are told.

This book is not an attack on my parents. I love them both. It's just a reflection of their and most people's attitude to life.

Have you met people like that?

People who will accept everything as it is. They will say and repeat phrases like –

'That's just the way it is.'

'There's nothing you can do, I just accept it.'

In England we have a saying, 'It's sod's law,' which basically means that it was meant to happen and was going to happen, so just accept it!

In other words, people accept their lot in life and allow themselves to be guided by Zoomanity into a life of reliance.

In addiction terms they call it 'dependency'!

Sex, Politics, Religion, Tea & The Zooman

As I write this book in Asana Tea Shop (thank you for the wonderful tea) in Santa Cruz, California, I have a conversation with a total stranger. We speak for a while about things, just general things as strangers do.

And then I did it. I broke a rule of Zoomanity and began to speak about religion. Actually he raised the issue. I replied to him about the hypocrisy of religion (not God) and its involvement in governments and how they actively promote their congregations into wars (for example), to kill for God and country.

Of course this conversation was longer. Maybe it was me going on a little too much about religion. (Don't read this wrong, I have a strong faith but I also accept most religions dishonour what they claim to believe in.)

Do you agree or are you getting that feeling of mentally closing down as you read this paragraph because I have mentioned religion?

Don't worry, that's normal in Zoomanity so don't give up reading just yet.

Back to the guy. He went silent, in fact so silent he actually got up and left with one simple statement: 'Have a good day, man.'

I had gotten out of line. I had questioned things. It made him uncomfortable. He walked away.

Isn't that how Zoomanity has created the zooman to feel and think about discussions of any depth like this? To be resistant and uncomfortable with open conversation, which leads to the shut down of the mind and shut down of the brain, which in turn creates resistance. Why do we comply?

Do you ever ask why? If you replied 'No,' maybe it's time you do ask why.

Are you one of those people who usually say things like, 'You give it too much thought'?

I've seen and heard that time and time again in life. This has happened to me time and time again. Has it happened to you?

'Shut up, Alan. You give it way too much thought, you're too deep'.

I'm sure you have or maybe you don't talk about subjects like these? Why not? Who said you should not?

Question everything; it's your right to. Right?

Conditioning is the behaviour of the repeatists. (The repeatists are those who simply repeat what the have been told. They blindly accept everything as a fact and repeat the same to family, friends, and anyone who will listen. This is all part of Zoomanity.)

Want a classic example of repeatist behaviour? OK, four words: 'The Earth is flat'.

Sounds ridiculous to us now in the 21st century but that 'fact' was repeated time and time again for decade after decade. Why? Because people were *told* it was flat. It's that simple. Their refusal to change their thought based in scientific fact might sound outrageous to us but it highlights the power of the repeatists and conditioning.

How about the Earth is the centre of the universe? Until Galileo proved that wrong with his use of *factual* science proving the Sun was in fact the centre of our small universe.

This created uproar in society to the extent Galileo faced persecution, court, judgements, and spent the rest of his life condemned as a heretic because of his 'factual findings'.

The repeatists don't like change. It challenges them at every level and they will fight even the truth.

You've met those who won't shift their views, right?

They are stubborn despite the facts and show a concrete-like refusal to budge!

Let me break this down a little more because it places the groundwork for your own exciting escape from Zoomanity.

Were you ever told by someone in your life that there are three things you never talk about in public (and in lots of cases private):

- Sex
- Politics
- Religion

Now of course you've heard that, who hasn't?

But the real question is, why not?

Who said we shouldn't talk about subjects such as religion? Stop right now and ask yourself who actually said this?

How did you react? Did you really ask yourself the question?

Can you see how repeatism and conditioning work in Zoomanity? (I will explain Zoomanity in its bigger picture in the life of everyone as this book goes on.)

Try this. Next time someone says to you they don't talk about religion or you shouldn't talk about religion, ask why and listen closely to the answer or lack of answer they offer to you. You'll be surprised at what answers are offered.

You're not doing this to catch them out; you are simply doing it as an exercise to prove a small point about Zoomanity and its very subtle controls over your life every day.

I mean, let's be honest, aren't these subjects – sex, politics and religion – some of the most critical subjects that makes yours and everybody else's world go around?

Nations are won and lost on the basis of these three subjects, yet we are told not to discuss them.

Then there's the darker side of life, the lies and deception and good things of politics: is it really for the conversation of the elite so they and they only can make the decisions that will affect my life and yours?

Think about this. Are you happy with the way everything is being run in your country right now?

Think about the ongoing controversies of so-named powerful leaders working for you the tax payer, the everyday guy on the street (there's another – why are we called just an everyday guy on the street?), and the mismanagement of taxes or information that you have given permission to these leaders of Zoomanity to use properly.

You have given them something huge – your trust. Do you think it's being abused?

How about investments that you made for life – for the day you finally retire and give up work forever – that failed or simply never delivered the promises that were made maybe twenty, thirty, or more years ago, and local authorities and even expenses scandals that have been experienced.

Local counsellors using your cash to have extravagant parties or stay in the most lavish of hotels whilst away on a conference. We vote them in and they use and abuse their power (not all of course) yet we are told we shouldn't talk openly about politics. Why? Does the flow of information about this subject affect your life or not?

How do you feel about those things? Do you give them much thought or do you do as you're told and that is to trust them and leave them to it because they know exactly what they are doing?

This is how Zoomanity likes you to be. They like you to be passive, submissive, and placid to the extreme. The less you ask the more they can get away with. You can see that right? You have seen that in your life?

TV, media, and the constant gorge of dumbed-down brain food being fed to mankind create a subliminal insidious damage that most never see.

Again let's be honest here. Shouldn't we have open conversation about these kind of subjects?

Can you feel your resistance levels rising as you read these lines, or do you find yourself saying yes, it feels right we should question everything?

Yet it's a resistance, but to what? To the subjects or to deep engrained conditioning that has been enforced by who, by what?

Think about this. Why should any kind of resistance come into play here? Is this a natural thing to allow others to run, control, and direct every part of your life, or are you simply part of long-term conditioning that almost everyone is supposed to accept as normal?

Religion Is a Fact of Life

Religion cannot be blamed for all our troubles. Only those looking to manipulate the masses can be blamed for that.

Yet think about this: we are told we shouldn't support religion as it is the creator of all of mankind's problems. Is it? The fast answer you might say is yes. But the reality is that is a surface reply.

The reality is that if religions practiced what they preached their believers would be people of peace.

And of course, I have my own religious experiences that are pretty intense and spanned a period of over twenty years. I'll reveal a whole lot more about that later.

So here's another thought. Would the followers want peace or war? The answer is clear, yet we are told never to talk about subjects like this. Simple reasoning can quickly reveal how we are being manipulated and dumbed-down to an alarming level to ask no questions about anything.

Do you agree so far? I'm not asking you to agree, I'm simply trying to wake you with a very light shake to from the sleep most of mankind (and that's you) might be in right now. Is that OK with you? If so keep reading because there's more to come yet.

Even as I start to write this book (October 2010) there is a news report on the BBC talking about the massive waste in government cash and the money – billions – that could be saved.

A new government has just arrived in the UK and the first thing they have promised to do is look at the 'waste' from the previous government in power.

What they have uncovered is absolutely incredible. The new government have actually taken the steps of hiring one of the UK's biggest and most successful business moguls, Phillip Green, to investigate this personally. I watched him on the news going over a report that is totally outrageous in words I couldn't even write here.

To get to the bottom of the waste cash, Green went directly to the people providing services to the previous government. He interviewed previous government ministers and most of them couldn't give the replies that Green required to accurately complete his report. He questioned the spending of over a billion pounds. When he asked those responsible how this had happened no one could give a reply. It was a case of no one questioned anything. They weren't supposed to, and even worse, neither are you.

Isn't that interesting? I think it is. If it affects those in the know (the zoo keepers), it'll have an even bigger effect on the zoomans living in the zoo.

Do you think the truth of that report (like any other report) will come out? No, because if it did there would be rioting on the streets.

Do you personally ever question who said we must follow these rules and ask no questions? Be honest, do you?

Sex

And of course there's sex. We are told not to talk about sex, not in public anyway. Never talk about sex because it doesn't really exist, right? No sex, no human family. It's a fact (according to…?).

And isn't it incredible that partners spend entire marriages and lifetimes never once talking about their sexual needs from their partner, yet they *have* needs. They feel frustrated or otherwise, but can't and won't talk openly to their partner. Why not? Because the zookeepers have told us for decades and longer, you don't talk about sex!

The results are usually one of a few things: divorce, adultery, or total frustration that breeds long-term resentment from the afflicted partner.

In other words, a damned miserable marriage or partnership. Maybe you've had one of those relationships? Maybe you have one now?

Yet, we know that the statistics prove it and still we don't talk about sex. Why not? It's a human function, isn't it?

Now be honest. How did you feel reading about those subjects in short sharp order above?

Did you hope this book is *not* about politics, religion, or sex? Did you feel resistance almost stopping you reading or answering back at me firmly in your head?

That's a good thing. Well done, you are alive. Yet at the same time that raises an issue and that's what this book is about.

Why do we have so many rules, fixations, and deeply embedded and conditioned ideas of almost every aspect of how we are supposed to live our lives? Yet some or even a lot of them are for our own good.

Do we really truly question everything we are told to do, in depth, with an open mind and honesty, for our own or our family's sakes?

Just because Zoomanity said we should do it, is that a good enough reason to do it and blindly follow what we are told to do?

Or are you like millions of others who are starting to wake up from Zoomanity's grip and starting to ask more, question more, and see more to your life?

I encourage you to read and be open to the ideas within this book.

This could be the start of a new life for you. The shackles and bindings of Zoomanity could be about to fall from you so you discover more to your life and the simple escape you can experience from Zoomanity.

Let's go to the beginning.

My World of Zoomanity

Forty-eight years ago I arrived in Zoomanity.

Forty-eight years later I'm asking the question 'What the hell is going on in this place?'

OK, I know there are a lot of happy people out there, and I know there are a lot of unhappy people.

You see, at forty-eight years old you've done a fair bit of living. More than some, less than others.

I've experienced and seen human misery through divorced friends, bankrupts, house repossessions, lost savings, lost jobs, lost friendships and so much more.

Personally I've been through painful divorce, humiliating bankruptcy, the tearful losing of my home I built, losing most my family, losing self-respect, regaining self respect, huge career changes, speaking on global stages all over the world, being recognised on the streets as an expert, becoming a religious minister, losing my set-in-stone faith. There's more a lot more and I'll share with you as we go through this book.

Of course I've seen and had more than my share of very happy times! My four brilliant kids, building my own home with my own hands, and of course lots of other times.

I think if you're reading this you'll be nodding your head in agreement.

But I'm not alone, and I'm not the only person to share these experiences. In fact since the dawn of man we have all been feeling pain of one kind or another.

Do you know people, friends, or family, or are you yourself, going through pain and misery that feels like it'll never end?

If you replied 'yes' you'll be asking questions. So why is it like this?

Zoomanity Is Real in Your Life!

Like it or not, your life is lived in the powerful, silent, subliminal restraints of Zoomanity.

Zoomanity creates illusions, dreamscapes, the unreachable, and a fantasy life that will pain you to chase.

Zoomanity is genius at cleverly stripping away almost all characteristics of humanity — *your* humanity. I'll try to awaken you from their enforced trance.

Zoomanity restrains, holds back, silences, extinguishes dreams, and creates silent followers who follow without asking why.

Zoomanity is controlled by blind and brilliant human zoo keepers who plan and repeat and do as they are told. They give mankind a cage-like experience to live in and unless you behave, you will have huge restrictions placed on every aspect of your life.

Your humanity is slowly and masterfully being squeezed out from you on a constant daily basis. You are being dumbed, numbed, and manipulated in ways the majority of mankind doesn't even realise.

Being aware of what is taking place daily can quite literally change the way you think and feel about life. Your life.

When you become aware you'll experience a moment like a bolt, like a flash, like a jolt that will change your life forever — if you jump into the flow!

May I ask you a couple of quick questions?

- Are you happy with the way your life is right now?

- Are you happy the way your life has gone so far?

- Do you think if you had done things different your life could have been better?

- Do you feel it's too late to change things?

- Do you often look back and imagine how things could have been so different?

I know, I know.

Believe me, that can change, but you have to become more aware of why life is (or was) the way it is (or has been right now). These are the things you can't see in your life but you can feel the effect on your life from them.

Zoo Keepers and You!

The zoo keepers are clever, ever so subtle, so that for you to truly be aware of their seductive, manipulative and stealth guidance takes insight, brain power, thought, reasoning, questioning and discovery of yourself and an understanding of the bigger picture of you, your life, and your history as a human.

Don't worry, it's not complicated. The zoo keepers want you to think it is. In fact, they don't even want you to think!

I'll take you along a journey of my own discoveries and personal escape from Zoomanity and relate some stories along the way to show you that despite any age you and your life can easily be reconfigured, taken apart, reconstructed, rebuilt, and maximized so you too can gain personal, inner, deeper happiness.

Think about this:

- Almost everything you do today and everyday is controlled by the Zoomanity.

- What you feed your mind and body daily is carefully planned by Zoomanity.

- How you create your lifestyle was not an accident. This is how Zoomanity wants you to live (exist).

- You are no longer a human as humans are meant to be. You are the zooman living inside the manufactured and controlled place we shall call Zoomanity.

And the reason for starting these writings with you is very simple.

- To make you aware of Zoomanity.

- To help you become awakened from the embedded trance of Zoomanity.

- To help you to become more conscious of the choices you can make each day.

- To help you unlock, uncover and release your true humanity.

- To inspire you, to motivate you, to give you scope, excitement and hope for your future.

- This is all about your own eventual escape from Zoomanity.

Zoomanity and Its Beginnings

I wonder — was it ancient Nimrod, mentioned in the Bible, who started Zoomanity? He had this idea that mankind would be better in a controlled environment. The reality is that he wanted and felt the need to control mankind so he could have power over them.

Nimrod's idea was very simple. 'Build me a city (Babel), build me a tower that reaches into the heavens and I will give you everything you'll ever need to live a happy life.'

I think this is the oldest recorded city in written records. From those early days we have the same (modernised) version even today. The principles are identical.

- Create an environment where the human feels they get almost everything they want and need in life (by telling them what they need).

- Remove all decision making but at the same time allow the human to think they have made the decisions themselves.

- Keep them in fear of loss, fear of pain, fear of being alive, fear of life, fear of almost everything.

- Remove their sense of humanity by creating a production-line-type of human.

- Feed them what weakens them, and when they feel the weakness offer the solution fast and simple.

- Give them places to live based on what Zoomanity determines is the ideal way to live. This way they reach for what they conditioned to see as the 'ideal'.

- Give them enough food to eat, feed them processed foods packed with addictive agents so when they taste they buy and buy and buy. When they get bored with that addiction create new ones then sell with masterful marketing practices.

- Create subtle desires so deeply placed within them that are designed only to make them believe they need those things to be happy.

- Make sure they live a life of dependency on the Zoomanity from birth to death.

- If they step out of line make sure they always know there will be a price to pay.

- We create the zooman, we control the zooman. We are Zoomanity.

It's clever, very clever.

Animal-Human-Zooman

Let's illustrate this idea.

Have you seen those big bears, like a polar bear on TV or in a real zoo, pacing back and forth, or facing the corner and banging their heads against the wall? (You can see this on YouTube.)

Some times they lose all of their hair or at least in big patches, they lose teeth and lose all sense of direction and ability to be the one thing they truly are – a *bear*.

The bear of course is not alone in the zoo. The king of the plain and hunter to the hunted, the mighty roaring pride of lions, also lazily sit in their fifty-by-fifty-foot cages and wait for food to be thrown to them.

Like a 21st-century human getting fatter and lazier hitting remote controls and dialling for a pizza, the lion shamefully is treated and starting to look the same. A watered-down version of an animal, anything but real!

The cheetah, the fastest land animal, has almost forgotten how to run, and even then how can it reach its sixty-mile-per-hour speed in a tiny cage?

The huge, herculean elephant that is used to digging huge holes, ripping out fully grown trees and swimming in fast flowing rivers barely walks in his compound as he awaits the keeper hosing him down from a rubber hose as they both stand on the concrete floor that is 'easier to clean'.

Right? You've been there right and seen them. You of course know what I am talking about.

Zoomanity.

To run the animal zoo successfully it takes organisation. It has to be clever, well planned in every detail. The one thing that can't go wrong is to lose control of the animals. To lose control will be an absolute disaster for the zoo.

It's critical that the animals be kept in a relatively happy but passive state at all times.

The thing to remember is that the animals were wild. We have to remove the wildness but allow them to *feel* wild. The zoo keepers have to try and replicate the environment each animal comes from. They have to work out what food the animals eat, and make sure they get the same kind of foods. Most of the time this isn't possible – bringing a truck load of gazelle to feed to the lions wouldn't go down well with the public! So a mix of chemically engineered food stuffs are created to give them the same nutrients as the animals would get in the wild (really).

Yes, they get raw meat also if that's what they eat. And yes, they get others things the animals get in the wild.

They get everything apart from the one life-giving ingredient.

Freedom.

Freedom to roam, create, to chase for dinner and be what they are – wild animals.

For example, according to information available online, elephants have been known to walk at least fifty miles daily!

Lions also cover mile after mile. They stalk, chase and hunt down their food. Monkeys jump from tree to tree, swinging, playing almost flying through the air.

Do you realise how far a whale will swim in a day or in a year? To take that and put it in a tank with no fish, no plankton, no anything apart from water – who does it depend on for survival?

- Giving a lion long grass in the zoo doesn't keep it wild.
- Giving a cheetah raw meat doesn't make it wild.
- Giving a whale water to swim in doesn't make it wild.

Alligators, parrots, snakes – every animal does what wild animals do, and that is live a full life based on their natural instincts.

I might not be a zoo or animal expert but here is what is obvious. You take the 'wild' away from an animal and what does the animal become?

No longer wild, that's for sure.

For instance, I didn't realise until I researched it that it's rare for a zoo elephant to live beyond thirty years, unlike the *seventy* years they live in the wild.

Most zoo animals with few exceptions live the length of life of an animal in the wild. Sad but true.

So here's the zoo concept.

People like me and you get a thrill from seeing what we think and are told are captured wild animals in captivity.

The animals become passive and the keeper is in total control. The keeper is now in a position where he can get these wild animals to do almost anything. If they refuse to do it he can hold back their food. In the worst case he can even end their life.

Let's look closely at this scene.

The public get to see the wild animal up close. The keepers and sellers of the zoo keep everything to their benefit.

The animals?

Well, if anything happens to the animals the zoo owners can always go to the market place and get another. The animals are nothing short of a commodity.

- Most animals do not and cannot live out their life potential.
- Most will not live like wild animals need to live in the wild.

- Most will suffer in silence or be silenced whilst suffering so the public doesn't see the reality of caging a wild animal.

- The animals forget how to hunt for food and create existence.

- They forget how to roam, walk, pace, run and even mark their territory.

- They forget how to *be animals*.

They have now become show pieces with the label of 'wild' above the door. They are anything but what they were designed to be. Just shells of their reality as wild animals.

Now look I'm not making any claims of being an animal expert because clearly I'm not an expert in elephants of any other wild beast.

I know nothing about zoos. I know some are brilliant. This is not meant to be a critique or review of a zoo or anything to do with zoos. This is a simple illustration against what *humans* have become. The reality and dreamscape of Zoomanity and how it has stripped most of humanity bare of our natural humanness just as it has stripped wild animals of their wildness in a zoo of their animal-ness.

Wild animal becomes zoo animal.

Human becomes zooman.

Wild Man to Zooman

When you look at man you are seeing a shell, a thin veneer of what a man really is, what he can become, and what his potential truly is.

Now here's what is interesting for you, for me, for humanity lost in Zoomanity.

The animal in most cases can be led back to freedom under the right conditions. Yes, elephants, cheetahs, and monkeys – almost all animals – can be led back into their wild state if the conditions are right.

In most cases the animals can stop being zoo showpieces, escape from the zoo, and go back into a wild state where the animals become real wild animals again.

The zoo animal never lost its wildness.

The wildness is still deep in there. It was simply covered up and concealed by man's manipulation. It can be masterfully recovered and uncovered.

This is relevant to you right now and your own escape from Zoomanity.

The Zoomanity Show

Jim Carrey made a brilliant movie called *The Truman Show*. Did you see it?

I think it illustrates the clarity of Zoomanity rule over man.

If you didn't see *The Truman Show* you must order it on my recommendation and watch it.

Truman's life appears to be totally, absolutely wonderfully perfect. He is happy with his wife, his car, his home, and his whole perfect life.

Until one day he tries to book a flight so he can travel to far and distant lands, see the world, and treat his wife. He goes into the travel shop and asks the travel assistant to book his flight so they can go. The travel assistant acts strange and gives him all kinds of crazy excuses of why she can't get him a flight.

He leaves frustrated that something so simple can't be fixed yet at the same time he suspects something is wrong. His inner being can feel it.

As the movie continues there's a lot of things take place that continue to raise Truman's suspicions that things are not quite right.

Awakened by an Old Volkswagen

Then there's a moment in the movie when he drags his wife into his car. He is going crazy at this point in the movie and he asks her to look behind the car at a certain time. Truman knows that at the same time each day without fail an old yellow Volkswagen will drive across the street. He's right, when it happens while his wife is there he goes hysterical.

Now he *knows* something's not quite right but he isn't sure what it is.

Next Truman goes on a driving frenzy around the town to escape from his impending insanity (awakening to Zoomanity). Each street he drives up becomes blocked. Each turn he tries is stopped. It feels like the whole town is stopping him from getting anywhere and he now knows it.

This is the point where Carrey, who is brilliant at playing Truman, goes totally crazy.

Remember that Truman has no idea the town is part of a reality TV show and all of the town are actors.

He decides to follow his feelings. He does some crazy stuff and knows a point has arrived, he knows, he is now conscious and awake and senses deeply that nothing is as it appears.

He can feel the fakeness, see the falseness, and has awakened to his own reality of happiness and life itself.

The people of the town all know the truth. They are paid actors. They tell him he is going crazy. They try and restrain him, hold him back, pin him down even send in an old friend to have a long talk with him about how great life is where they are.

Zoomanity's Favourite Tool: Fear

I didn't mention that life for Truman is on an island. The island is surrounded by water. Truman is terrified of water since his dad drowned in a boating accident when he was just a child.

He doesn't know that throughout his life his fear of water has been reinforced to make sure he is kept in place and restrained from taking action and moving out.

Because of his fear he refuses to cross the water by going over the bridge. The bridge is the only way off the island. Even looking down on water terrifies Truman.

This is his greatest fear, yet he knows his life isn't what it should be and it's looking like his only way to escape is over the water.

Finally the decision has been made: come rain or shine, hell or high water, now is Truman's time to escape from his insanity (the movie's Zoomanity).

He decides it's time for him to face his biggest fears, water and boats, and get on a boat and sail out of the town where he lives. This is a huge thing for Truman. (Of course using fear to control mankind isn't new and has been used for millenniums to keep mankind in its place.)

Truman Escapes from Zoomanity

Truman creates the perfect escape plan. He takes massive action despite being terrified of facing water.

Within hours he is on a boat and sailing into what he thinks is freedom.

But there's only one thing Truman fears more than water: a storm at sea.

That's what takes place. A storm arrives out of nowhere, almost drowning Truman.

He survives and climbs back aboard the boat until suddenly when he is miles away from land something bizarre takes place.

Truman's boat crashes into what appears to be a wall in the middle of the ocean.

Not only that, but when Truman leaves the boat the water is shallow. Not what you'd expect in the middle of the Pacific Ocean.

He climbs out of the boat. The water is shallow. He walks to where the boat has stopped and feels a wall with his hands. He sees some almost invisible steps and climbs up them to find a door.

Baffled and confused, one thing has become true for him. The life he had been living was a lie. It was controlled and it was under the influence of everyone and anyone part from his own influence.

Truman had escaped. He had escaped from a life that was never his own. He was met by the TV show producers (yes, his life was a show almost like Big Brother), and they share the truth with him.

Now and only now could he start his life again based around his own feelings, wants, needs, and more. He had escaped a Zoomanity. He was the caged exhibit people paid to watch.

Again, if you haven't seen it go get *The Truman Show* with Jim Carrey (even if you don't like Carrey, as he seems to have a love or hate appeal. I love him.)

The Truman Show is a good illustration of control of a single life, or so it seemed, when actually the single life the show tried to control was the one life that had become awakened to the realities of life. The masses who watched the TV show called *The Truman Show* – they were the real victims.

Movie and Reality

Now I know the above is a story and a movie, yet for most the movie is reality and has been reality for millenniums.

Man, woman, you, me, we are under the direct influence of Zoomanity and I'll take you on a journey next through my own experiences in Zoomanity.

Almost everything you aim for in life, want, chase, desire, reach for – is it part of Zoomanity?

My Life in Zoomanity

Growing up was tough.

Mum had three kids by the age of twenty. Dad was always looking for more ways to earn cash. Home was a flat on the first floor and life was tough!

Life for my parents was a constant battle against poverty and a lack of knowing what would be on the dinner table on a daily basis.

We were all born in Leith in Edinburgh, Scotland. It was very working class and well below the poverty level.

Dad had a start to life that was pretty unusual. Not long after he was born his father left home and simply vanished for the next nineteen years. Not long after his father left home so did his mother. My dad was raised by his grandparents.

My dad relates the problem this caused him mentally, of always having a feeling of not being sure 'who he was'. As a young boy his real name was James Smith but so he could be identified as his grandparents' boy he was named unofficially James Bogie. Dad tells the story of the confusion with his name and how it affected his thinking as a child.

When he was nineteen years old, dad finally met his father in a pub in Leith.

My dad's granddad said to my dad, 'Come over here and meet this man'.

Dad went over and his granddad said to him, 'James, this is your dad'.

Dad accepted him for who he was and they remained friends until my granddad Smith died.

Dad's mother would appear every now and then, he rarely saw her and never lived under the same roof as her until the age of 21 years old when leaving the army he lived with her for just a few months until he found his own place.

Twenty years later, dad's mother and father re-united and had another child!

I can only imagine the mental affect this had on my dad over the years.

I really didn't see a lot of dad when I was young and can barely remember those times when he actually played with us.

He worked long, long hours, doing what was expected, getting jobs, getting paid and surviving with his young family. He like other men would do almost anything to feed his family. Finally he became a window cleaner. In those days cleaning windows in Edinburgh carried a high mortality rate as the window cleaners would scale up the outside as far as possible up the five-, six-, or ten-story old stone tenements and office buildings.

Beyond the reach of the ladder the window cleaner would have to do the rest almost in the style of Spiderman, with no ropes, no safety for anything, and if you fell, death would usually be the result!

This was long before health and safety had even been thought about. It wasn't uncommon for window cleaners to fall to their death. Dad had a few falls but unlike some of his pals, he survived – damaged, but survived.

Dad told me the story of one of his friends who was cleaning a window at the top of a building. His friend accidently pushed a loose stone lintel on the roof of the building. The stone lintel came away and fell to the ground five stories below. Sadly his friend's coat was hooked to the lintel, and this pulled the friend down to the ground with the large stone landing on his face. His face was smashed but he survived the fall. My dad told me the story of how when he went to see him in St. James Hospital in Edinburgh, his face was like a huge black plum with no features showing. Sadly he later died from his injuries.

This wasn't working for my dad, it wasn't a career, it was always survival.

Yet he was a rule player by default. He lived the way he was supposed to live, did what he was supposed to do, cared for, worked for and aimed for like he was supposed to do. That was expected of course, there was no other way – only the Zoomanity way! Ask no questions, just carry on at all costs.

It wasn't dad's fault; he was following the ways of old, the repeatism from others that has been passed on.

'This is the way, follow it'!

Mum was more than busy with her young children. Mum's family were pretty stable and almost middle class. They actually had a shared garden that was shared amongst the four flats but a garden all the same, which believe me was pretty unusual then. Despite her middle-class family of course mum still had to make it on her own.

Mum worked hard. She was also very smart (still is). To make more cash to feed the kids, mum worked for an egg and dairy farm called

Pinkie Mains in Leith Edinburgh. She delivered dairy products in an old grey Austin Mini van.

Often I would go with her as the youngest out of the three kids and can clearly remember the smell of eggs, butter and stinking milk that would be dry and sticky on the floor of the back of the van where I would excitedly sit amongst the crates until mum would stop and open the back doors.

I would jump out and mum would walk up to the doors with the orders. I just stood at the side of her with a big smile on my wee red Scots face.

As a four-year-old there's not a great deal you can do, but the householders, although just as broke as mum and dad, would always give me a penny or two, so by the end of the round I would feel like a very rich wee laddie!

Mum would of course always insist on looking after my cash (strangely, I would never see it again).

It really was a tough life of survival for them. Never any money. Never any clothes. Never any food. Never any hope. Never any anything.

Life in Edinburgh was all about struggle, never enough of anything. But that's how it was and that's how it was accepted. Work hard, die hard.

Mum Begins to Wake Up!

My mother was and still is a smart woman. She started to wake up. Me and my three siblings were lucky – my mum had the vision and wisdom to see the futility of their existence in Zoomanity, their Zoomanity. They played by the rules but the rules were killing them! Mum could see if things remained the same, it couldn't last. It was just too hard, too painful, too much of an endless struggle for her husband and young family.

The passed-on chain of what was expected, what was repeated and what was common was about to be broken. Life had been really tough for them so far so change was coming and coming fast!

It took someone in a long family line of the same old stuff to do something new and break the repeatist patterns, snap the expected chains that had been handed down from their own parents, and lines of families that were expected to do the same as before with no questions asked – the controls and instilled fears of the zooman.

You know: just do what everyone else does, follow the line, behave and work hard for your survival.

My parents, pushed ahead by my mother, finally took the plunge and broke away from their family, friends, culture and whole life.

England — A New Improved Zoomanity

In the 1970s they were the first to break away from the regular tradition of what everyone was supposed to do. Hard work, drink hard, stay broke, stop moaning, question nothing.

They had to go against family resistance of breaking out, moving away and starting a brand new life in another country.

They broke the chain for the sake of their children and future generations. I don't think they saw that then but history reveals the reason and results of a break like this. When we used to go back to visit family in Scotland I always found it interesting that they were all doing the same thing they had always done because that is what you are supposed to do, right?

We would visit relatives doing exactly the same as always. They were looking ravaged by ill health, drink, and smoking. Heart disease was rife, early death was common, and it was frowned upon to make money of any kind.

Mum's and dad's commitment to breaking out and changing the lives of their children had an impact in ways they could never have foresaw. Their escape from their own Zoomanity.

Reflections of Mum, Dad & Zoomanity

I'm sitting here looking back, sharing a momentous change my parents made in their own early escape from Zoomanity in the late 1960s early 1970s. They could have done what they were told by everyone and stayed there.

'Do as you're told'. 'Ask no questions'. 'It's always like this'. You know the things that are said to us when we start to awaken and realize things aren't quite right? Yet the truth is that we all do what is repeated to us from someone else without rarely asking why. Someone tells us we should do things a certain way. We do those things almost without questioning. Yet they are repeating a behaviour of a previous generation and generations before that.

This doesn't mean they the individuals are wrong. They were simply doing what Zoomanity wants them to do. Zoomanity is clever and clear. It's a silent system that holds us in a grip of never asking why.

Zoomanity Fear

Zoomanity instructions are based around fears. Break the rules and you face dire consequences.

Yet when we break the rules and follow our inner voice, the directions of Zoomanity begin to sound ridiculous.

Fear is the biggest constraint in Zoomanity. They love to use it.

Don't believe me? Watch any news channel anytime of the day.

What do you have fears of?

Losing your job? Terrorist attacks? Swimming in the sea and a shark eats you? Using the underground and a bomb goes off? Flying and it crashes? Losing your pension? Losing your savings? Losing your home? What others will think? What your friends will say? What your husband will say if you tell him what you really think? What your wife will say if you are more honest?

Fear is the biggest control of Zoomanity.

Find out your fears and face them. My parents were terrified of moving, breaking away, doing something out there, different, new, and breaking the chains and asking questions.

They asked the why and the what and the how, and finally awoke to the reality that the old way of life was going to destroy them.

How about you?

Me

So I was born.

February 1963 I arrived. No big deal, just another kid in another town.

I was born at home in the back room of 15 Hope Terrace, Leith, Edinburgh. Nothing special. Poor, cold and below average.

Like I said the environment was a tough one but of course when you are a kid as long as you have food and love, it always seems fine. No one had anything so there was nothing to be jealous about. It was just a life we accepted.

Want to Eat? Go Catch Fish!

One of the early childhood memories I had was fishing in New Haven harbour where me and my older brother Steve would go down to the docks daily to see if we could get any fish or crab or even get an undersized lobster from the local trawler men.

This was actually a place we would have to go almost daily to try and catch food.

Steve looked after me; after all he was five years old. I was four with no front teeth and a blunt fringe!

We'd walk the half-mile over to the harbour, past the corn mill and eventually past the fish market then into the harbour.

We would walk to the steps near the lighthouse then out would come the string and safety pin with metal foil so the fish would be attracted to the shiny metal like the scales of a small fish.

On a good day we would actually find a real fishing hook to use. To do this you had to scour the cold wet stone floor looking between all of the cracks until you found a hook. These were always much better to use but still hard to tie on a string.

One after another my brother Steve and I would pull out small fish (around four inches long) and throw them into the bag. We would spend hour after hour doing this.

Our only snacks would be what we called the cauli-bucki (winkles), which were the living snails from the harbour wall. We'd simply pick them off the wall when the tide was low, pull out the snail with a pin and gulp. Chewing was not allowed!

On a good day we could even return home with a crab, some big fish or a lobster from the fishermen.

This takes me back to the day my dad didn't really know how to handle a lobster properly. He brought it home and decided to keep it alive in the bath until we were ready to eat it up. The bath was filled and the lobster dropped in until the time would arrive for cooking.

Dad entered the bathroom. I can remember a scream then dad running out with a lobster fixed firmly to his finger, screaming 'Get a knife, get a knife and cut it off'. I had a crazy vision of mum chopping dad's finger off but of course it was the lobster that was facing certain death here, not dad's finger.

Life in Scotland was just life, nothing more. Survival and staying alive. When there was no food we had to find it. Neighbours, family, or go catch some fish – it was that simple.

Death Wakes Me Up!

This was still back in Scotland. Where I lived things at home could be sometimes unusual. We often had a spiritual things taking place at home. It wasn't unusual for my mum to have a medium around. She also made claims of powers from another source (I don't mean the electric board either!). If she had these powers they certainly never helped her with her cooking!

I'm not sure who the first dead person was that I saw lying in a coffin but it was common that the dead were laid out at their home for all to come and pay last respects.

As we went into the house it was pretty happy but solemn. All were talking and drinking whiskey ready for the big party, I suspect where stories of life and lots of drink would play its role.

I slowly sneaked my five-year-old head around the corner to see a long box lying on the bed. I tiptoed only to see the end of the dead person's nose popping up. I got a little closer and saw her face. I remember thinking is she dead or asleep? If she were dead or asleep why was she wearing her glasses? It never made sense. It felt strange.

I left the room and later went back to my Granny Smith's flat with my family. It was there I couldn't stop thinking about the dead person lying there – still, dead, lifeless. Where had she gone? Was that it? Would I also have to die?

She had lived a life in line of Zoomanity. Worked hard, got the nice place, stayed in line, and now vanished, back to the dust. Where had she gone? Had it all been worth it? What was her legacy?

Do I Have to Die?

Back to Granny Smith's then. She looked very Scots, always smiling and smoking and always chewing her gum. If I asked her what she was eating she always said it was 'working gum' and children didn't work so they couldn't have it. She looked striking with her big grey curly, almost afro hair, never a cigarette out of her hand with a big yellow stain running up the front of her hair from the smoke.

I asked my Granny Smith this question: 'Do I have to die as well, granny?'

'Yes' she replied.

I fell to my knees, put my face flat onto the big chair my granny would sit on and cried.

To this day I can remember the feeling of being born to eventually die. It never felt right, it never felt fair, but it was a reality. I cried on granny's big chair knowing that one day I would die.

Looking back this feels like my first real spiritual moment that would shape a huge twenty-year part of my life in the future. Was death part of the curse of Zoomanity or just the inevitable outcome for all men?

Life Is Short — Zoomanity Knows That

So if life was to be short was I to hand my life into the hands, the thoughts the rules, the directions, and the regulations of Zoomanity – or was I to create an experience that would fill a book, that would read well and inspire those I was to eventually leave behind?

We arrive here on the planet. We are given a life to experience and enjoy. We will face sadness, happiness, stress, and all kinds of travels and journeys in the process.

It appears almost all the way though our lives we have something, someone telling us, shaping us, moulding us into their perceptions and conditioned beliefs into what we should be.

Do we live a life that fulfils us? Do we make and create our own decisions or are we fooled by mass media messages on how to live the perfect life?

It seems interesting that the majority of people moan about life and what they don't have yet they rarely do anything about it due to self-imposed constraints of Zoomanity.

How about you? Would you like your life to be different but are in fear of change?

Our reality is death comes to all, your life is time and that time willrun out at some point.

Death comes to all yet it feels an escape from the clutches of Zoomanity is possible through listening closer to what we are saying to ourselves.

Man on the Moon and Beyond

Dad walked in.

'Boys, wake up! A man is going to land on the moon!'

It was around 1am I think. The date was definitely July 21st 1969. My brother Steve and I were allowed to sit on the sofa and fall asleep.

We had a large black-and-white rental TV that had round dials to carefully tune in each channel, a wooden surround that I had etched my name into with a pin, and the speakers had a lightly woven cream-coloured cloth stretched over the top of them.

Dad shook us both and said 'Wake up, wake up' to me and Steve. We excitedly woke up. Dad said, 'He is just about to get out of the space ship'.

Of course we knew what was happening, a man was about to land on the moon. Everyone had been talking about it for ages and following it on TV. Now the moment had come.

We both quickly sat up, went over and sat right in front of the TV on large cushions on the floor about two feet from the screen.

Space, planets, rockets – we were watching a spaceship and a man in a spacesuit actually on *another planet*. My mind was spinning I remember it so clearly. Will aliens welcome him or blast him like in so many 1950s B-movies? Who knows, but whatever was about to happen we'd see it live as it actually happened!

And there it was. He kind of hopped off his spaceship into the dust and uttered the ten immortal words 'One small step for man. One giant leap for mankind'.

Seconds after hearing that, there arrived six more immortal words: 'Get to bed both of you'.

I lay in bed for ages after thinking about this event. It was huge even for a small six-year-old boy.

God, Aliens & Spaceships

Aliens, planets, spaceships, spacemen, moon dust. Would they find life on the moon? Was it really made from cheese? All I knew was this was something that made me think about life and God even at the young age. If God exists why would he make life on Earth only? Is there life on other planets? If so where? Do we have a monopoly on life? I had no idea but here's what I do know in reflection.

The whole thing was an incredible achievement by man, no question. Yet if mankind can do this they can solve everything. Zoomanity was getting even stronger, more powerful, gaining followers but creating those that were becoming more awake at the same time.

Suddenly my world as a child had grown, expanded and stretched my thinking. Where does space end? What is a star? Why the moon or any other planet? How did they stay there and not float away?

This was the start of my own mind expansion, the intrigue, the curiosity, the fascination with more than what I could actually see. This proved to become a pattern in my life.

The etchings of the zooman versus the human were being born. I had no idea what was to come, yet an awakening in 'life more than this' had certainly been kick-started.

Moving to England — New Zoomanity

Dad was to spend his next thirty years in prison.

We eventually moved to England, and dad got what he thought was a dream job. The big attraction for him and for his young family was a good pension, a steady job, a home, and regular money. The changes in life were to be gigantic.I remember it so clearly. The car was packed to the hilt, all three kids were in the car whilst my pregnant mum drove us the long road to Cheshire, England where we had a new home waiting.

This really was a great escape and, looking back, an early escape from Zoomanity for my parents.

Their restrictions from the old ways had been smashed. Mum had taken the lead and we were on our way to a new life! For mum and dad, this was big, very big!

I recall the old Austin Cambridge car mum had (dad never drove) had a huge hole where your feet went under the carpet on in the back. As we drove along Steve and I would lie on the floor in the back of the car with the carpet rolled back as we dared each other to reach down and touch the road as we drove along the road at sixty mph.

After several breakdowns in the big old car we finally arrived. I can even remember getting out at 4 Bentham Road and running upstairs to quickly claim a big bedroom.

At this young stage in my life I had never seen a place so extravagant. We had separate rooms up and downstairs. We had a real house with a garden. Before we lived in a cramped modern tenement at B59 Fort Place in Leith. This was the second floor. No one had a garden apart from those on the ground floor flats. Now I had a garden to play in with my big brother Steve.

Looking back today it almost looked like the Truman show I mentioned at the start with all houses the same, all ideals the same, all the men worked the same and breaking out was almost like breaking out from prison for the men folk!

As a young boy of seven years I loved it. I felt so different to what I had for the first seven years of my life.

We all had pets now. In the old flat we lived in no one could have them. We had the luxury of walking out the front door and being on the ground floor rather than running up and down the stairwells of the flats back in Scotland.

This was also a time when we rarely saw our fathers and a drinking culture of the prison warden estate took over the lives of many of the men.

Bullet in the Head

In those days the Irish war was still raging. Dad took a dangerous job with huge payments in Belfast, Ireland for a period of time working in what was called the Maze Prison. He came back after being held at gunpoint and just inches from having a bullet in his head from Irish Nationalists.

This move was a critical part of the new life not just for my family but for future generations like my own children. After all, if my parents hadn't broke the chains of what-should-be-and-ask-no-questions, maybe my own life would have ended with drug-infested jail sentences or ill health and drink problems like so many of those we left behind.

History shows there are times when the escape must take place – the moment of realisation when someone in a family can make a huge difference to future generations. My parents did that. Of course at the time they and no one else realised it, yet looking back it was a revolution to make the dramatic move they made.

Another escape from Zoomanity was breaking the chain!

Scottish Boy, English School

The downside was this: can you imagine being a seven-year-old with a thick, raw, hard-to-understand Scottish accent, being thrown into the culture of English kids?

From day one I got bullied, not just by the kids but by the teachers who would continually laugh and mock my accent.

Not a day would pass without a challenge of some kind. I liked it when Steve was around because he would protect me. The main problem I had was that I started in the last year of infant school and he was now in the junior school next door. This led to me being punched, kicked, laughed at and bullied by the English kids – and the teachers.

Teachers! Mr. Sneddon and Mr. Hartley, despite your continually mocking me in front of the class, I forgive you both.

It would go like this.

One day Mr. Hartley told me to come to the front of the classroom.

'Haggis (or Jock), come to the front of the class please!'

(Yes, they really did call me haggis or jock. These are nicknames for Scots by English.)

They would force me to stand in front of the whole class and say words with a rolling 'R' in there. Words like 'wo'r'ld' or anything with a big R in the word. If you have heard a Scots accent you know this is a strong sound that can't be written on paper.

The result was great laughter from a class of thirty-five English kids to be followed by a day of mockery in the playground. Not great when you're just seven years old, alone, and in a foreign country.

Of course as I look back over this time this would lead to me getting stronger and stronger, never weaker; yet the bullying was tough for a kid.

The Zoo Says Reject Change, Push Away

It's interesting how we are programmed to react to an alien object or in this case a foreign or Scottish boy (me) arriving in the class.

The Zoo has conditioned us even as kids to reject, mock, and push away the new object. It really wasn't the fault of the kids; after all, kids will only repeat the repeatists, in their case their parents or adults around them.

The sound of an accent that is different, or the look or actions of someone or something different seems to provoke, highlight, or aggravate the switch that Zoomanity has installed inside us. Why? Isn't a human just a human or do we have to look at others that flick these switches and act the way Zoomanity has programmed us to react?

Wouldn't the world as a whole be a better place – a stronger, united, and happier place – if we could look at ourselves and ask ourselves how we react to others when they are clearly from another place?

Wars are fought over cultures, accents, and ways of life. Even the Scots and English have had their fair share of slaughter against each other. These are the old ways of Zoomanity – days of past times that have no place in humanity.

Fundraising and Saving the Planet

TV has its good side.

Biafra.

I can remember. In 1970 suddenly all over the TV we were seeing images of the dead and dying. Small. Frail. Thin black African kids and adults beaming into our family homes through the screen in the corner.

Can you remember the Biafra disaster? We were force-fed a stream of humans looking like the living dead, children close to death with huge bloated bodies because of civil war. Those images were transmitted all over the world by the power of TV. This was one of the earliest global things I personally recall.

I watched the politicians on TV. They looked well fed, in fact overfed. They lived in big houses with lots of expensive ornaments and finery, as did the church leaders.

Yet here's what I saw on my TV screen. Dead people and a lot of dead people, rotting stinking unfed corpses dead and dying on the streets of a country I have never even heard of. Arms like sticks, bellies like balloons, tears flowing like rivers amongst the blood and filth of war.

The nations like to show how much they cared yet the reality was people were dying. Is this how Zoomanity cares for its followers?

It carried on of course, it was still on TV daily for what seemed weeks and it looked like not really any one of the governments were helping.

A campaign to help was launched on TV.

Nine-Year-Old Saving a Life

At the age of nine I took a decision.

I decided to invest 50p (I think it was this amount – I honestly don't recall) of my own cash each month to educate and school a child until he was sixteen years old.

I tore out a response form from the newspaper and filled it out with my name and details. I asked dad what he thought. He smiled and said, 'If you think so, do it'.

A few weeks later I got a large envelope in the mail with a young black Biafran boy's photograph and a hand written note from him thanking me. His name was Stephen. I did that until he was sixteen years old. I never got to know him but I did know this: If a nine-year-old boy could make a difference to another man's life, give him what he needs to progress in life, why could Zoomanity not do the same?

Zoomanity Abuse and Control

This is a feature of Zoomanity, of course. Create massive fear within mankind so the zooman has to continually look to their chosen leaders for a way out, for help, saving, salvation.

It felt wrong even to a nine-year-old. It feels wrong now.

How about you? How does the way mankind behaves feel to you?

Not only was Zoomanity allowing the death and abuse of humanity but it was busy reshaping, moulding, fabricating, deceiving, and guiding man into deeper and deeper misery.

The mass of Zoomanity was surging and flowing towards more and more control with misery mixed in. I could see it even as a nine-year-old. The rules and zoo keepers could also see it but they were doing nothing to prevent it. This was a big lesson in life, certainly for those suffering but also for myself as a young observer. No one was coming to save these people. They had to save themselves or the alternative would simply be death!

My inner character, the man I was to become, and impending escape from Zoomanity were building and growing fast. I was unaware but each life experience was shaping and moulding me. It was taking me and making me into the man I am today.

Your life is doing the very same for you. Are you preparing for your own escape from Zoomanity? Do you question or accept everything? Will your salvation come from another or come from yourself? Zoomanity demands everything – even life if that's all you have to give.

1976 and Punk Rock

Am I an anarchist?

I liked the idea of green hair. I also liked the idea of questioning everything.

The Sex Pistols punk rock band arrived and they looked almost insane with their self-cut, green, red, blue hair and rag-like clothing.

They had been quickly banned on TV for songs like 'God Save the Queen' and 'Anarchy in the UK', and their album *Never Mind The Bollocks*, and just to really put the perfect stamp on their anarchic approach against Zoomanity and the music business they were gloriously dumped time and time again by their record labels.

It looked to me as if they were having fun doing their own thing while questioning lots of mainstream subjects – and I wanted some of it.

The Queen of England's Royal Jubilee of 1977 was approaching. The whole country was preparing for a huge street party. Not the Sex Pistols – they were questioning everything!

People with the guts to say what they thought. It felt right at the time to me. After all, we had been through glam rock with Marc Bolan and David Bowie, Mud, and other soft rock bands. This felt like perfect timing for me the teenager who was constantly questioning everything.

Schoolboy to Punk Rocker

I went upstairs and found a really old suit of my dad's. I asked dad if he would ever wear it again so I could have it. He said no and asked why I wanted his wedding/funeral suit?

I never told him of course. I took it from his wardrobe and started to do what any good punk rocker did and that was rip it to pieces and then repair it with safety pins, paper clips, and badges with rebel slogans on.

I can remember declaring myself 'punk'.

Well, part-time punk. During the day I was still Alan the school kid. At night I almost did a full moon werewolf change into this punk rock rebel monster.

Zoomanity Mocking the Punk

I remember the very first time I left the house in my punk regalia. It was a Friday night to go to the Croft (a local village in Cheshire) disco. This was in the village next door, which meant I would have to get a bus and be seen by everyone.

I put on dad's old far-too-big suit held together by safety pins. I had chopped my 1970s long hair off into a home-cut spiked look and then carefully walked downstairs hoping mum and dad wouldn't see me leave the house.

A creak and mum shouted, 'Are you going out now?'

I replied, "Yes".

Mum knew how I would be dressed. She said come in here and let me see you. Reluctantly I popped just my head around the door. To my horror there was a bunch of women sitting there with mum. Mum told me to come right in and let everyone see what I was wearing. I did just that to a volcanic roar of humiliating laughter from a bunch of zooman women who were living their lives as they were told would be right for them by Zoomanity.

I'd Started to Escape Zoomanity

My own personal escape was really starting to take place. The more vocal, more open rebel had started to surface. The opinions, the thoughts, the voice, the ability and knowing it would be fine to voice my opinion despite almost everything telling me it was wrong, shouting at me and trying to silence me. I was just a kid, of course.

I went from my house to the bus stop and then onto the bus. Of course more humiliation. A fifteen-year-old kid doing exactly the opposite to everyone else because he was ignited and inspired by the Sex Pistols and the thought of punk rock and doing his own thing.

I got bashed up at the disco but that's another story!

It feels such a teenage thing to write here but this was something in my young life that allowed me to speak up, stand up and become aware that I really didn't have to do all that I was being told about life. I didn't have to look and dress like the masses, I didn't have to stay silent like I was told to, I didn't have to keep my head low. Even at such a young age I could revolt in a small way against Zoomanity and the law of the masses.

Lets Start a Band!

The next step up from that felt obvious: Start a band! So then came my new punk band, myself as singer, Andy Booth on guitar, Robin Pinkney on lead, Nigel Long on bass, and Dave on drums (of course like all good bands we fired and hired so not forgetting Kenny Dennis and Will Jennings).

This was it, what would I name my band?

I saw a photo in a music magazine of a punk rocker trying to look identical to a member of the Sex Pistols named Sid Vicious who had stabbed his wife Nancy Spungen to death and then overdosed, ending his life in New York.

The headline under the photo called him a Clone Youth.

So my band was born – Clone Youth.

We did what all teenagers do: think we are amazing despite being average, played gigs, caused a few riots, and had fun.

Punk rock was another turning or awakening moment for me. For the reason it taught me self-thought. I could voice my opinion even in the face of the majority. I could feel I was being myself despite everyone else telling me I looked stupid or was wrong. I could do things no one else dared to because I was willing to put myself out there and actually do it.

Dad and others told me I would never get a job looking like that. Of course I got jobs. They told me no one would deal with me talking about anti-racism, world poverty and other injustices like the Falkland's War. Of course they did – deep down they admired my young approach because they would see the part of them that was suppressed and locked away.

They had become victims of Zoomanity itself without even realising; I was on one of my early steps to being awakened into action although I didn't know quite what was coming.

It taught me it's OK to say what I think and feel. Why not? I like others was here to experience life, enjoy, rejoice and go against the grain when I felt it was right to do just that. No one likes a voice, something different, the truth, or uncomfortable moments with words. I was learning and learning fast. Zoomanity was losing its control over this young man.

Do you feel like your voice has been silenced over the years? Did you want to stand up more for what you felt was right but never did it and took the action it needed to make it happen?

It's never too late. You can escape Zoomanity at anytime. It's a choice you must make. It's a moment when you awake, become aware, and can no longer hold back.

Even I began to be silenced, as you'll read later. Then something strange happened around the year 1979.

The Punk and the Clergyman

'Right – who wants to get baptised? asked my mother.

'Why' I asked, 'would a sixteen-year-old punk rocker like myself with green, blue and red hair want to get baptised in a church I had never been to?'

Mum said if we don't my sister wouldn't be allowed to get married in the local church. OK, I said I would, but I was really not happy about it. It felt wrong.

The day arrived. We all headed down to the local church called New Church in Culcheth. Mum and dad dressed in their finest. My siblings looking smart and my young seven-year-old brother also had joined the family. Mum had insisted I dye my green hair nice and brown for the day, so I compromised and did it black and yellow!

The church felt cold, alien, empty, and almost businesslike. In front of the Smith family getting baptised (and paying for it) were around five or six babies being held by their parents.

The vicar picked each one up one after another and baptised them. I recall in each case he asked the baby's name – he never knew any of them at all.

Then of course it was our turn.

First came my small, annoying, and very overweight at the time seven-year-old spoilt little brother Eann with his big smile from ear-to-ear. Next my older brother Steve, always smiling, always Steve. Finally my sister who needed to join the church so she could get married there; after all it was very pretty and would make great photos.

I stood and watched and kept wondering what is the point of this?

Of course then it was *my* turn. The vicar looked at me with a piercing judgment; I know he was saying to himself, 'I'll do *this* one – but *that* one is definitely heading straight to Hell.'

He ignored me.

It all felt very wrong at the time. Afterwards we all (with the other new Christians) went to the pub where the older ones and parents silently got drunk to celebrate their conversion into a new faith minus seventy pounds a head or whatever it was.

I remember that day so clearly, not the exact details but as a day that really stuck with me even until today. My feelings were that the man of the cloth was doing his best and yet it was so insincere, so routine, so nothing. Although I am sure he did what he did with the greatest intentions it felt a long way from anything I would consider to be God.

This whole thing stuck with my mind forever. Again I was faced with the question of if there is a God, then why does he allow this mess we live in? Why does he allow war in the Falklands and racism and all the other terrible things that were being fed into my young mind from Zoomanity media channels?

My reflections are that this is just another tool in the world of Zoomanity. Not as much as decades or centuries before but a way to silence the masses.

Marx said that religion is the opium of the masses. I know it's often quoted. Was it? Is it? Maybe it used to be, I don't believe it is, not anymore, there are far more decisive, destructive ways to control the mind of a man. Control his mind and you create the zooman. Caged, restricted and unable to even think for himself. More on the new opium further in the book.

The good news is I survived and moved on to a life where I would gain more and more control over all of my thinking and actions.

The above was my first real venture into religion as an experience. It felt like nothing but made me think deeply about mainstream faith. If a nation were to follow leaders like these, the nation would be weak, insipid, and easily knocked over. Yet it was clear that a faith of some kind could also create a powerful human that would be hard to shift in a moment when strength was really needed from a man; after all, history proved that people have died time and time again for a faith. Was this Zoomanity playing with the follower?

It was clear the clergy didn't have any power, they never led in a way that would make transformations in my life.

It felt cold and insincere for me.

It made me think but I wasn't ready for the trappings of religion as I understood it then.

I Went from Pink to Yellow

I climbed out of bed, looked in the mirror and I was yellow. As yellow as the skin of a banana.

In panic I screamed. My mum called up to me and asked what's up? I told her I was yellow. She told me to come down and immediately told me I was jaundiced and had to go to hospital right now. I cried thinking my life was about to end. Operations, amputations, invasive surgery was what my mind was telling me was awaiting.

The reality is what was waiting for me was six months bed rest.

I went into hospital with bright red hair and bright yellow skin. Maybe it was an alien that had inspired me during the moon landing. I certainly was looking like one.

First call was the doctor's surgery. He saw me, backed away and immediately called and ambulance. I have to say he left the room pretty quickly. I sat there until the ambulance arrived. Was I dying? I had no idea. I just didn't know if yellow meant death.

They rushed me to hospital and put me in a room that was sealed with a warning sign on the door with one word: INFECTIOUS.

One by one the doctors would come in fully covered with long white coats and breathing masks, treating me almost like E.T. in the movie. I was scared and getting more scared by the minute.

Doctors appear to have a habit of prodding a lot, saying a little and murmuring even more. Then of course they leave the room in silence shaking their heads.

Finally another doctor arrived, asked me to turn to one side whilst he stuck a huge needle into me and then drained me of some blood.

Again in silence, he left the room.

I was left alone to think and chew things over for a while. I had no idea what was wrong but I was thinking look at me just sixteen years old and I'm dying. I think the fact that I was a different colour to everyone else on the hospital didn't help.

Of course I wasn't dying. Two days later the doctors arrived and removed all the protective barriers. By this time my banana yellow was more of a sunburn yellow. I wasn't quite sure which shade went best with my bright red hair.

The doctor said with his forced smile, 'Good news! You're not infectious.'

Here's me – bright yellow, lying alone, lost and over thinking on a bed about impending death – and he thinks it's good news!

After a week they sent me home with six months bed rest and plenty of water. I had contracted hepatitis.

I do remember during that time I had nurses, counsellors, and doctors coming to me daily, and all of them asking me about my drug abuse.

Apart from a nasal squirt, which isn't exactly life expanding, I'd never used drugs in my life.

Yet they couldn't get away from their Zooman script. Hepatitis equals drugs. He's a teenager so he must be lying. He looks different so must be taking drugs. Keep asking and pressing him, he'll give up in the end. This is the repeatist behaviour that asks the same old patterns of repeat! We see kids on the streets that look like kids on the street, yet the media paints them as criminals on the street.

Some things never change. Zoomanity wants you to believe the script that most kids are a menace to society and should be feared. I know people who have their home surrounded by CCTV cameras 'just in case teenagers come', despite the fact they live in crime-free zones!

The hospital saw me during that time as just another teenager to be suspicious of. They were playing out the same old script they had been taught.

This episode of illness had a huge effect on my life then. My initial reaction was to understand my life can end at anytime, so what am I doing to make sure that doesn't happen? On the back of that I started to look at natural therapies during my months of bed rest. That's when I discovered a book of my mother's that talked very openly about mysterious energy lines know as meridians in Tai Chi.

Now you need to know I wasn't a reader. I really hadn't read a book from start to end. I had walked away from school at sixteen years old and had no formal examination certificates, so reading and learning really wasn't on my agenda, not in the traditional way. I always believed that you learnt what you needed to know at the time.

This was one of those times. I needed to know about health and how to be better at looking after it. This book landed on my lap at the time. I read it, all of it, and applied it to my own life.

And to be honest it felt a bit 'out there' at the time so it really suited me and the life I wanted. I always resisted the rules and the formality of everything. It always felt wrong that we had to do the same as everyone else was doing. My young years had started to see Zoomanity for what it really was.

So after reading the book on natural energies and learning about invisible powers and energies within me, it got me thinking. For some time I would go to my bedroom in the evening, lock the door, and practice what I'd read in this book about these meridian lines that would run in a pattern all the way through the body, and then I'd practice a specific meditation that was taught in the book. I would go into a deep state of thought around 11pm and come out around 3am very easily.

I kept my bedroom door locked during this period. I knew that most people I knew including family would not agree with my new discovery that I was enjoying practicing, or they would do what people always do and that is say it's weird.

Maybe my experiences as the Scottish kid in the English class gave me a fear of being mocked so I told no one at the time.

I have no idea if it worked at the time but what I did understand was that there was something outside the world of conventional thinking. These were ancient Chinese practices that talked about energies that run through all men and are connected to the universe. This when I was around sixteen years old in 1979.

Of course this goes against the rules of Zoomanity. They don't want anyone doing anything different or out the ordinary. We see even how mainstream medicine rejects natural remedies as outlandish and unproven, or they simply laugh them off.

Yet we have incredible healers like Deepak Chopra and thinkers like Bruce Lipton who have shown that healing can take place from inside without drugs.

The reality is Zoomanity wants us, feeds us, almost forces drugs on us. Why and why do most people never question why?

I had a friend who is dead now. His name was Gary. I believe medicine killed him. In his mid-thirties he started on anti-depressants. He soon began to have serious hallucinations and paranoia. This led to *more* drugs being prescribed to counteract the effect of other drugs. This went on for years. He went from a happy musician to a paranoid train wreck of a man. Thin, grey, gaunt and always ill.

At forty-two he dropped dead of a huge heart attack.

Gary never seemed to question anything. If they said take it, he took it. I believe this killed him.

Question everything!

When we do question things that the mainstream or Zoomanity accepts, they resist us. This is designed to make us feel uncomfortable and uneasy. When we feel like that we also want the feeling to vanish so we fall back in line if we are weak!

They laugh, they scoff, they try and do everything to pull us into line. Who's line? The lines, the rules and the boundaries of a self-imposed Zoomanity.

In hospital I had been through another moment of becoming aware, becoming awake, and understanding that just because I couldn't see it (meridian energies) it didn't mean it didn't exist.

Also my illness made me realise that life is fragile. It can come and go. By sixteen years old I had seen and experienced death of family and even peers. One girl from school having a heart attack at the age of sixteen, dropping dead on a flight to Spain. Another school friend being killed on his motorbike.

Life seemed so short even at a young age, who was to live it? Me? Or would I allow others to live it for me?

Talk of Impending Apocalypse, Drugs and Faith

During my punk rock phase I became more and more sensitive to global issues. In the UK we had an organization known as Campaign for Nuclear Disarmament (CND). Bruce Kent was the founder – a preacher becoming a pseudo-politician (like most preachers do – glory before God).

This awakened me a little more and took me down a path of human fear. The fear was: What if another country attacked us with a nuclear bomb?

We even started to have TV shows on how to survive the attack when it took place.

Looking back, it got pretty ridiculous. I even recall a TV show that showed us how to survive a nuclear blast. We were told; 'As soon as the bomb goes off or is about to go off, get a sofa, turn it upside down and place it next to the wall. Then lie between the wall and the sofa. This will increase your chances of survival'.

Probably the most ridiculous public campaign for survival ever! Massive areas had vanished in a second in Hiroshima because of these bombs yet we were being told to lie under a sofa. How gullible do the media and Zoomanity think we are?

That did raise the question – are sofas and mattresses really nuclear bomb resistant? If that was the case why are government ministers digging into mountains of hard stone thousands of feet down to survive the blast and fallout, yet they tell us, the masses, Zoomanity, that when they get into a fight with another government a sofa will be our saving grace at the point of impact!

Around the same time this experience forced me into asking more questions on life itself.

Why was man so cruel?

How could another man shoot a man in a pointless war?

Why is the world so wicked?

Would the world actually end one day and one day soon?

And many, many more questions.

Did I believe in God at this point of my young life? I have no idea if I am being honest in looking back, but I had seen lots of things going on that let me know there had to be some kind of invisible powers.

When I was seventeen years old in my punk band we had just finished a gig and then we all decided to go back to Nigel's house because his mum and dad were out – hence we could drink smoke and be loud!

For fun we set up a spirit-inducing Ouija board on the kitchen table. There was myself, Dave our drummer to my right, John, Kenny, Andy, and Will around the table. We had set all the letters around on the table, gotten a glass, put it upside down. We had no candles to finish the gothic replica room so we put a battery torch in the corner turned upside down to give us some light.

We started.

'Is there anybody there?'

Nothing happened.

'Is there anybody there?'

Again nothing happened.

'Is there anybody there? If so make yourself known,' we repeated with small giggles laced with a cold fear.

Then suddenly the glass with our fingers on it began to move around the table.

We all looked at each other like teenagers do, smiling and wondering which of us was actually moving the glass.

It started to spell out word letter by letter.

P E T E R

So the name of this spirit was Peter. Of course we all still felt one of us was directing the glass. I looked at John, John looked at me, we all looked at each other. Every hair on my body was standing upright. It felt cold, chilling and terrifying yet I wanted to keep going.

Then something like the following words were spelt out by the glass:

T H E R E

I S

D A N G E R

I N

T H E

R O O M

This was the point where we all started to freak out and keep asking each other who was moving the glass? All denied moving the glass.

Dave the drummer was seated at my left hand side.

Suddenly John shouted, 'Look at Dave!'

Dave was in a trance-like state with masses of what looked like phlegm pouring from his nose and mouth. Apart from Dave, everyone jumped and pulled their hands off the glass.

The glass began to rock violently back and to, then suddenly it flew across the table with a violent force and smashed into a thousand pieces against the wall.

At this point Dave collapsed into a semi-conscious state while at the same time punching the table screaming 'Don't let me die, don't let me die!'

In sheer panic we phoned a hospital and then an emergency crisis centre. They both thought we were a bunch of kids playing a prank at 1:30am in the morning. We decided the best thing to do would be to drive my car to John's house and take Dave there. His mum was good with weird stuff – she always seemed to know a lot of answers to nothing in particular.

When we got there and told her the story she simply said, 'Yes, he's possessed,' and then carried in drinking what looked like whiskey and smoking what looked very like a joint!

We all stayed awake all night long with Dave who cried for the whole night and talked about suicide.

From that day Dave went from being a clean cut guy to drug user and was never the same again.

That reminded me again – just because I can't see something with my physical eyes doesn't mean it doesn't exist. After all I can't see the wind yet does the wind exist?

I was learning a lot and seeing a lot of things taking place in my small world. The world was telling me this kind of thing didn't exist. The world of Zoomanity was telling me to rely on them. They were holding me in fear so I had to rely on them in a dependant manner.

Zoomanity was also behaving in a way that showed an utter disrespect for human life with threats of war. I was also being told that spirits and invisible forces never existed and can't exist. The punk rock scene was atheist in its manner, with very anti-religious songs. This led me along a similar path of thought. Looking back of course it was more anti religion than anti-God! Yet the fact remained that I was seeing something invisible, powerful and real in front of my own eyes taking place.

Just a reminder, this book is not about politics or religion. I am simply trying to relate to you how I was shaped into my conclusions today and my views of the controls, the repeatist behaviour the conditioning imposed on mankind by Zoomanity.

And if you feel your resistance grow as I talk about these subjects, that is good. It shows you are alive. It shows you are thinking, but more importantly it shows you are being challenged at a very foundational level.

Accept your challenge and see where this all leads for you – please!

Experiences like these took me on a quest for some kind of bigger, deeper faith but I didn't know this yet.

This also led me to do something I had never done in my life before: praying to something, somewhere in secret, away from mocking, on a regular basis.

Next step – I decided to become an ordained minister!

God Knocks on My Door

If there is a God then prove it, I would pray.

This part of the book is not about my faith or past. It's about allowing you into my life so I can share with you what shaped the conclusions I have come to in my life so far.

Conclusions of Zoomanity and the life of this zooman.

I want to ask you to suspend your resistance to faith for a moment. The reason I ask is a conditioned pre-judgment usually rises within others when I talk about my fundamentalist religious choices and pasts. You'll see why in a moment. Keep reading.

I started to read an old King James Bible. The old English made it very hard to read and understand.

In fact I became so convinced that there must be more than what we had I began to sleep with this old book on my chest hoping maybe an answer would come.

I asked my dad about it. Was it worth reading? He said it's good, read it and take what you feel is good.

I tried for months to do that but couldn't get past the old English. After Noah and the Ark I kind of gave up. It was just too heavy for me to read.

At the same time I began picking up books of all kinds of faiths and reading them. Islam, Catholic, Methodist, Adventist, Baptist, Animist, Shintoist, Christadelphian, Mormon, and literally dozens more. I kept this all very secret to start with.

Then one day I was in the attic at home looking for something and I found a small book in the corner under an old box. The small green, old and battered cover had the title *Is This Life All There Is?*

I opened and began to read it. It covered a lot of subjects I had already been through including death, spirits, God, and more. I wanted to know more. Eventually this led to me studying the Bible intensely with Jehovah's Witnesses.

This became a life of five meetings a week, and reading the Bible and other study materials almost every hour of every day. It was intense.

At the time, I absorbed it like water onto a dry sponge. I had a very strong thirst for spiritual things to come into my life and was ready to accept something.

I had so many questions and yet so many answers were coming out for me. After a while I took the decision to go through full immersion baptism and dedicate my life to Jehovah and serve his son Jesus.

This re-ignited my biggest fears, which went back to my younger days: rejection, mockery, and opposition from others. They came thick and fast.

This created fierce opposition from most of my family. My ex-father-in-law told me on more than one occasion my faith was worse than the Nazi faith and I should be lined up against a wall and shot. On another occasion he told me that he would rather I be an alcoholic than having a faith like this (you guessed right – he didn't like me).

The reactions from family, friends and total strangers were just as strong. During this period of my life I was threatened with death and faced threats of violence, threats of relationships breaking apart. I could reveal more but maybe that's another book.

I did this for twenty years. During that time I became an ordained minister. It taught me lots of disciplines. It helped me become a strong, strong man who understood what it was to stand firm in the face of any kind of opposition.

I mean who can say they had read the Bible from start to end at least half a dozen times?

The Bible gave me some control in my life that punk rock had removed. It showed me the answers were far bigger than a riot or street movement.

It also taught me to make a stand in what I truly believed in at the time. I mean, how can you stay sat down at a wedding of three hundred people during a toasting? You can imagine the reaction.

I was spat at, verbally abused, kicked, punched, laughed at and shouted and screamed at in public. If I could do this I really could conquer anything in my life.

Now one thing I want to say is this: Around 2005 I drifted from that faith but I always loved what it gave to me, the strength the power and conviction to become what I am today despite intense, fierce and at times violent opposition.

I remember an old friend called John Dagnall at my church telling me this: 'Until your faith is tested you don't know how strong it really truly is.'

This was from a brother who had been to prison for his faith in the 1950s.

Can you imagine walking from door to door talking about faith? Can you imagine standing in a city centre talking to passers-by about faith? Can you imagine walking through drug-infested housing estates, being threatened with death, spat on, mocked and publicly humiliated?

I did that for twenty years.

My own reality was that twenty years later I wasn't fulfilled at all. I found that being a minister gave me a life full of judgement. I would harshly judge and I was harshly judged by others in the church and out of the church.

You have to remember this was an extremely fundamentalist Christian faith. At the stage in life I was at, it had become almost impossible for me to carry on. I no longer got what I needed from the meetings. I resented judging others and others judging me. I resented brothers who weren't doing what they should be doing yet were happy to rule and lord over others.

I made the decision to leave. Slowly, like a small piece of driftwood leaving the shores, I drifted into the distance no longer connected to the church and faith that had served me for twenty years.

My family hated me being a witness. The strange thing was they then hated me *not* being a witness. This taught me about human resistance to change of any kind. Where did that resistance come from? Did I have the same resistances? Do I resist change or embrace change? The life lesson here was huge.

The other thing that was interesting during that period was the way Zoomanity teaches others about other things like faiths. Most people make a decision about a faith like JW based on what another has told them or repeatist behaviours.

Time and time again for twenty years I had people telling me what I believed. They would say things like, you don't believe in Jesus do you! I would say yes he is central to my faith. They would reply, no you don't! It would almost feel like a game whilst speaking to house holders.

This highlights the repeatist patterns in Zoomanity and how Zoomanity narrows our minds, controls our thoughts and make decisions for us despite our asking them not to make any decisions for us. Subliminal teaching at every level. Had even I spent twenty years repeating?

Our decisions and reactions, or statements we sometimes make to others are rarely our own. The opinion is usually automated in its outcome. We say what we know and we know what we have been told. How much do we question? Zoomanity wants you to question nothing.

Now I know exactly how most people feel when they read this so I want to really say here I am not saying any faith is right or wrong, I am simply asking do we make our choices and decisions based on what others tell us or do we make our own informed decisions?

A strong faith served me well but it had another effect. It was the effect Zoomanity has and that is to take and make life decisions for me. Almost everything I did over that long period in my life was based around the decisions that had been built into me with my faith.

I came to realise that to create a happy life, decisions must be taken by myself and no one else. When decisions are passed along to others, the result is usually not what we want. It's usually based around what someone else wants. We live our life based on something that was almost always passed along the lines with no questions being asked about the source.

Zoomanity wants to do all of the thinking for you. It wants to keep your scope of thought on anything narrow.

Being a Bible student gave me two valuable tools in my life:

1. To listen to others and to serve others.

2. Question everything – time for a change!

Let's Build a House

I always had an aversion to the mainstream. It never felt right. How can others decide what is best for you?

By this time I was living in my second house with my first two boys and first wife. It was a small English cottage with everything we needed.

It was nice, but I had a real thirst to build my own place.

At this time it was 1996. I had done and achieved quite a few things in my life so far. Things were good and steady yet I felt I'd be happier if we had *more*.

Big house, big cars, big everything. Isn't that what Zoomanity tells us is best for us? Don't most of us buy into that ideal?

So in 1996 I fell across an old farming building that really needed to be torn down and rebuilt.

Actually I'll share a small secret here that I haven't touched on in this book so far. The law of attraction had always been active in my life. Almost everything I had dreamt about had always arrived at some point. Cars, homes, or other stuff. I had dreamt about converting an old derelict barn for years. Here it was and I was suddenly going to own it. This was the law of attraction before the mainstream decided to label it and sell it as another teaching or new faith!

Back to the new house. You can imagine the horror on my family's and friends' faces when I told them I was going to move my kids and wife out of a beautiful home into a caravan that would have no running water, no drainage, and be parked in the middle of a mud-covered field surround by sheep.

All I could see in the wreck was the stunning home. All *they* could see was a total wreck of a building that was currently home to a cow, a horse and two tractors!

So early 1997 we moved out from our stunning cottage into the caravan and the build began. Almost everyone told us we were crazy! That made me want to do it even more! I really believe that when the masses are going one way the obvious thing is to go the other. Who is leading the masses? I like to lead myself!

Anyway…

I had to face a silent, disapproving opposition from my family. I had to also face opposition from my 'brothers' at the church I attended.

Despite the pressures of taking on a project like this I can look back on it and see this as my early stages from breaking away from Zoomanity.

By this time child number four arrived – my darling Lily – and life was absolutely full-on at this point. Four kids, running hairdressing salons, over sixteen staff, building my own house, and being a full-time religious minister was taking its toll on me.

I felt the pressure to say the least! I really wanted, needed and thirsted for change.

Looking back, by 2002 I was at a silent snapping point. Yes, the home we had built was stunning and our lives were beautiful with new cars, holidays, and four incredible kids. But the pressure from Zoomanity, although self-imposed at this stage, was absolutely huge. I felt alone, unsupported and drifting. Communications were always blocked and this led to a surge and eventually an explosion.

Deep down inside I knew this was not what life was meant to be. I had everything any man could want yet it wasn't enough for me. I wanted out of the trap of Zoomanity. The problem was that I was alone in this quest.

The grip of Zoomanity was becoming clearer and clearer. I wanted out of everything and I never felt I could share my thoughts with anyone close; after all, I had experienced a life where I was told I was too deep, thought to much, and should get on with it.

Sound familiar? More repeatism from Zoomanity. Think of nothing, ask no questions, and work until you die.

Not me!

I'm a Writer.
No, You're Not!

I wanted to be a writer but had no idea how to write. I had walked out of school because it always appeared to be academic (obviously) so I avoided it.

I had jobs, lots of them. Cleaning windows, handyman; but my first real job was a landscape gardener. Eventually I became a hairdresser. It had been a hobby of mine to cut friends' hair since I was around fifteen years old.

I got fired everywhere so I had to open my own salons. I was a salon owner for seventeen years. I was ready to move on from that; I got to a stage where I hated it because dealing with staff became just too much to deal with in my life. My back was getting worse and it was pressure on top of all the other pressures I had in my life.

I was really pushing through into being a writer of sorts.

At that time, by chance I started to get jobs as a copywriter. Business came in thick and fast. I was working fast! I was getting a lot of new clients, working alongside some top entrepreneurs, plus I had the honour of being guided by my good friend and early writing mentor, the hugely respected writer Michel Fortin. (www.MichelFortin.com)

At this point in my life I still had hair and beauty salons. They had all been going really well and I was seen as one of the best hair cutters in the region. I even had clients who would fly in to see me four times a year from as far away as Spain!

When I told my family I was selling up my salons and leaving hairdressing they totally thought I was going crazy. In a zooman way they never let me forget I was just Alan the hairdresser.

On the back of building a reputation as a hot-shot copywriter, invites poured in, one after another, to travel all over the world and speak from stages in Asia, Australia, New Zealand, Europe, and USA about the subject of creating sales copy for businesses and training others to do the same.

This sounds like it happened fast. It did. I knew at the time it would.

After nearly twenty years slaving in my salons I think you'll understand the appeal it had to me.

Speaking from a stage was nothing new to me. As a hairdresser I had spoken to many salon owners on behalf of cosmetic companies. Then as a minister I had been trained very well to speak in public and share information with a large audience.

However, the kind of speaking I had been used to doing was service based.

Suddenly I was propelled into an arena where the number one priority was to *sell* as much as you could to the people in the room.

The first questions to be asked by a promoter is 'Can you sell?'

Now I understand fully that if a promoter has a series of speakers who don't sell, he or she makes no money. I always got that bit.

The bit I always struggled with was the idea to just make something up to sell, to just get those credit cards out and people running to the back. After all, I had spent the previous twenty years speaking as a minister from a stage and platform, sharing, giving, and serving.

So I went along with this way of doing business for some time. It never sat well with me. The whole concept of filling a room with people just to sell almost anything to them had a strong effect on my inner being. I hated doing it.

I also found it hard to stomach the fact that some of the very best speakers were spending cash on being trained to do speaking and to persuade by using subtle crowd swaying techniques at an insidious level.

I have to say I have seen some outlandish stuff sold from stages all over the world. Promises are made to those in the crowd looking for a better way of life. People are investing into the hope promised by speakers only to find out later they had been sold to by speakers who had themselves invested thousands into the 'art of persuasion'.

Let me say here I have a lot of very good friends in the speaking business. You know who you are and I honour the fact you are promoters of change rather than takers of cash!

This new world of take, take, take was a world I could no longer be part of. I took a step back despite the possibility of making tens of thousands selling hope and promise.

As I look back now this new direction began to fill the void that was left by leaving my previous faith and I was loving every minute of the gap being filled.

In my personal life and with members of my family we would meet people in the street whom we hadn't seen for a while. The questions we always ask each other are the same, right?

'Hi what are you up to these days, how's your hairdressing doing?'

I would reply, 'I'm a writer now'.

My first wife and other family members would sometimes say in front of me and the friends, 'No, you're just a hairdresser. Why do you say that?'

Can you imaging the embarrassing horror I felt when she and other members of my family did this? I learnt a lot from that about how people feel and resist change.

Yet life is made up of change. More on that later.

The reality for me was life was changing really, really fast at this point.

Did I have to be a hairdresser all my life because I had spent twenty years doing that? Was change not allowed? Why was change seen to be such a dramatic thing in my life when we are always surrounded by change in life itself?

I learnt that what some will call a huge change had a strong resistance by its nature. Why? Should I also resist the change in others?

Change felt good. My inner feelings were pushing me through the law of man.

No longer the constraints and rules of Zoomanity.

Life Destruction Crisis

I snapped.

They use the term mid-life crisis in a negative, almost laughable context. It's a term I favour and rejoice in today.

Think beyond the statement.

If a country is in crisis they pull in the greatest minds, brains, thinkers, and people to make sure it gets sorted and a solution is found fast.

I was alone. I felt alone and had no one to turn to.

In 2007 I finally snapped, completely snapped. This ended in divorce and the complete breakdown of all I had known all of my life. Twenty-seven years of life exploded almost overnight.

I lost my home.

I lost my family.

I lost my friends.

I lost my wealth.

I couldn't get close to my kids.

My own family had stood and watched the collapse of my life. (Not that I blame them for anything but when a family member or someone close clearly needs help, you go help them, some did, some attacked me and why not… Zoomanity conditions a reaction when a reaction is required, they reacted the expected way.)

Suddenly for the very first time in my life I was totally alone, scared and dying inside. I cried for six months, day after day, night after night.

I would sit on hilltops, sit on wet shores, sit in lonely houses, sleep almost anywhere, drive out in the middle of the night and sit in the total blackness staring at the stars for hour upon hour.

These were the darkest moments of my life. I truly felt my life was at its end, its completion for me.

Thank you to my brother Steve who was there for me at the end of a phone. He supported me, held me with his care, and never once judged me. His concern was for me his brother, not the situation I was going through.

Most of my family had now gone, apart from my parents and my brother Steve. I had left them. They showed no attempt at helping me through this crisis and no compassion. I even received death threats from one member of my own family.

My faith had now been abandoned and my brothers in my faith had abandoned me.

These were crazy times for me, the man. I attracted what can only be called crazy, unstable and destructive people into my life at that time. One in particular, lied, cheated, deceived, and stole from me. Why not, I was in a crazy place, and like attracts like. Looking back it was all obvious!

I learnt a lot from this. Zoomanity never shares with us the reality of relationships. After twenty-seven years I was alone.

My first fifteen years were with my parents' love. During the next period of life – until I was forty-four years old – I was in my only relationship. I had made a choice based on what I felt was the right thing to do at that time.

Do you feel a judging moment rising in you as you read this? How can you? Why did you? I never would? But the truth is I had spent years saying the very same repeatist phrases. Judging those I had seen going through troubled times yet suddenly here was I in a situation for which I would have judged another.

Life was teaching me a lesson and I was learning fast. Zoomanity and its assumptions didn't care. Zoomanity and its teachings, the sheep like zooman and its pre-built assessment, decisions and actions were all built on repeatists behaviours that were never questions.

Think about it.

Why would a man with a twenty-seven-year track record of good, caring, and loving suddenly do something that appeared to be so crazy? Does that make the man a truly bad person or is he showing a symptom of something much bigger?

Was this a symptom of Zoomanity and the pressure put on modern day humans?

Life was not turning out as per the Zoomanity plan for me. Those in the thick of Zoomanity are told not to think. Don't ask. Play the game.

My own Zoomanity game rules had been smashed but life was about to go crazy.

The Human Is Out — All-Out Crazy!

Can you imagine how crazy a wild horse goes the second he is released into freedom?

The barn door opens after years of being locked within four small walls. They open and he is out¾finally free to roam, run, and be what he really is: a horse.

That was me.

Was I still searching for my own salvation from Zoomanity from the self-imposed lifestyle that had been drip-fed to me over the years?

I had my first fifteen years with my parents, then the next twenty-seven years with my wife. The empty gap was huge!

I felt desolate but had time to think. This was a crazy, crazy, crazy time for me. Everything I believed and lived had gone. This was my own ground zero. No words here can share the pain and confusion I was in.

Condemned by many yet rediscovering who I really was.

It felt brave. I felt cruel to those I'd left behind. Shattered. It had happened and I had to carry on. No one was coming for me. It was me alone and struggling.

I don't and will never believe anyone changes. People always become what they have always been. During these release periods the person you always wanted to be but was suppressed comes to the surface and comes to the surface pretty fast!

Within weeks the changes are huge. Within two months the gap from who you were and who you now are gets even wider. Within three to six months there is no going back. The distance between the past and present is far to wide.

The thirst I had for spiritual food hadn't gone. I felt as though it still needed to be fed. I was hungry. I missed regular spiritual reading and feeding because it fed me at my core although I never missed the endless routine of it all or the judging.

This is where I went down a new path toward self-help, self-discovery and new age 'faiths'. I never looked for them; like most things they simply arrived and like most things in my life these days I embraced the experiences.

What an interesting place. It wasn't for me. The problem was simple. This was a group of people who had created a new faith to replace an old faith. These were proclaiming their non-God beliefs yet at the same time they were fixed so firmly to their new paradigm they refused to budge.

I met a woman who was searching. So was I. I attracted trouble… BIG trouble.

Her life would revolve around an adopted eastern (or any other) philosophy, mixed with almost anything that she read from new-age gurus.

If she read about raw food, all cooked food would be seen by her as toxic. It would then move on to drinking water from a tap – more poison. Publicly she would say eating meat will give everyone cancer yet she would always eat meat from my table in private where no one would see.

It was an on-the-surface, self-significant feeding habit created by many of this same group of people. She was an extreme example.

She would read a book, a new book, hear a talk, hear a new talk, course, or manual, and her views would change to an extreme. Then she would tell me the only way to start any day would be a colonic wash and then vomit.

If she were around others, she would become them. If she heard others speak, she would speak like them. Talk of purpose, vision and intuition yet this was a search that would always result in another search. This approach was hugely destructive and of course only brought its own end. She a deceiver at the highest level. Looking back, I deserved that at the time, I allowed it and it taught me a powerful lesson. This was the first time I met a human being lacking in real self. The first time I would meet what I would name 'chameleon-being' … someone that lacked in self anything so would take on the self of another. Devour, absorb, take all that is needed and move on to the next thing or person was her life. Greed and destruction, another trait of Zoomanity. The non-creative creates from the destruction of another.

This approach appeared to be pretty common in this world – following, doing, repeating, and acting out another role for the role they had left behind.

This was a new age-old page paradigm that always appeared to be people caressing each other's ears with talk of self-righteousness for the planet and themselves.

Another fallacy of Zoomanity as you'll see.

Not to say any of those practices don't have health benefits. They can, of course, but I smile as I think of my drunken granddad sat smoking his rolled-up cigarettes at the ripe old age of eighty-seven.

I've seen this all over the planet as I have given talks to audiences all over the earth.

Attraction of a Book

Then I had a strange experience.

Someone had told me to read a particular spiritual book. Maybe it was because of my firmly held beliefs as a minister that I resisted reading this 'spiritual' book for about a year or more.

I had thought about it on many occasions yet never been out and bought it.

One day I had a party. At this party there was a huge pile of wrapped books that were to be gifts. The books were all books that had helped, in the past, the person who was giving the book away.

At the end of the party all eighty wrapped books had been taken except a single book that was left on the table. It was for me and was handed to me.

I opened the book and it was the book I had been told time and time again to buy. It was the book that I had been thinking over and maybe reading one day.

Suddenly it emerged from beneath the gift wrappings and appeared before me.

I know you'll want to know so I'll tell you. It was *The Law of Attraction* by Abraham, Esther, and Jerry Hicks.

At the time this blew my mind, as you can imagine. Did I find this book? Was this book attracted to me? Did the book come to me? Was it sent to me? I have no idea but I was in no mood for another twenty years of fixed beliefs.

The above was a huge period of new discovery for me. People, ideals, beliefs, they were coming thick and fast, but the reality is they offered no escape from Zoomanity!

Amazon Trip and Real Humans

There were lots of things taking place over a short period of time. I had the opportunity to create a fund raiser for the Pachamama Alliance in San Francisco. They are active in saving the South American rain forest and its indigenous peoples.

Single-handedly I created a fundraiser in Sydney Australia and raised a huge amount over a three-day period. I then gave the cheque to the Pachamama Alliance (see www.pachamama.org)

On the back of this I received an invite to the rainforest to see how the cheque had been spent. I went into the Amazon jungle and spent fourteen days in Ecuador on a trip I'll never forget.

During that trip into the tribe I didn't realise until we got there that most of the participants had gone on the trip to meet the shaman and take the hallucinogenic root commonly known as ayawaska. Before I went on this trip I had been sent a huge pile of information on why one should take the opportunity to drink this root and ask the shaman for answers that would change one's life. This was a year I had done a lot of travelling with my speaking and initially I really didn't want to go. I finally went but never read a thing about the trip so had no idea that most people on the trip were there for a spiritual awakening with the shaman.

On the bus heading to the small airport named Shell (after the oil company) a man asked me what I expected from the drug and the shaman.

I replied I had no idea what he was talking about. He smiled and thought I was kidding. I replied not at all and he and some others went on to explain to me.

They explained they were searching for answers in their lives. After taking the hallucinogenic roots the answers would appear to them in the dreams, and then the shaman would explain the meaning of the dream to them so they could live a better more fulfilled life.

Were they repeating a pattern that kept appearing before me as my life was carrying on?

We finally arrived at the tribal Achuar village after a five-hour trek through thick jungle.

The arrangement had been made for the root to be ingested and the subsequent meeting with the shaman. That night everyone met in the tribal home of the shaman. It was pitch black. All you could see were faint outlines. The shaman himself was barely visible. The hut had a soil floor with mounds. The mounds were the graves of their family. We had to step over them. If felt very primitive to say the least.

The time finally arrived for the shaman to give out the drink. Almost everyone took it in search of their personal truth, their future, or their next steps to be taken in life.

After everyone had taken the root I was again asked if I was taking it. I replied no, thank you. I really never felt the need to search outside of myself for direction and after all I had been through I wanted to be my real self for a while at least!

I was then offered a tribal cleansing. I thought, well it can't hurt so I'll relax and experience it.

I was led to the shaman by my friend Lynne Twist. As I sat down all I could hear was a single voice tribal chant and dried tobacco leaves shaking around my head and body. There was smoke being blown on to me so I closed my eyes.

As I closed my eyes something very strange took place: a huge eye appeared before me, gradually getting bigger. I have to say it gave me a fright so I opened my eyes. The tiny shaman appeared as a black giant in front of me. I closed my eyes and I saw the eye, so I opened them again and saw the giant. My initial reaction was fear.

I kept it quiet apart from sharing with Lynne after the cleansing had ended. Finally I shared the story with her.

The next day we all had to go back to the shaman where everyone had to relate the dreams or visions they all had while under the influence of the root.

Each person one after another shared their dreams. All dreams sounded much the same. Snakes, eagles, condors, and long life.

Eventually they came to me in the hut. I said I had not taken the root so had nothing to share. Lynne spoke up and said I had a very important story to share.

Reluctantly I told to the shaman what had taken place. His reaction and the tribe's reaction was clear – something unusual had taken place.

I have to say here I'm not overly comfortable sharing this but I will. He told me this:

'You do not need the root. The giant is the tree the shaman gets his power from. You are a giant, you are a shaman. The eye is the wisdom of the shaman. You have the wisdom. You do not need the root.'

The hut was in silence. I was confused, as you can imagine. Then the stories of dreams carried on.

As time went on over the next few years my thirst for spiritual food continued and continues until today.

What I do know is this, wherever I have been on this earth, to the most advanced to the most primitive, people are people.

I had already spent twenty years of my life tied and bound in another faith. Self-imposed conditions, restrictions, and guilt-laden plans were holding back my bigger experience of my life itself. I really didn't want to get back into being told how my life should be run again. Despite carrying the name of 'new age' or other adopted labels my personal experience was this was more of a faith tied down in mixed practices, but practices that all the same had a lot of people in their grip. Some had walked away from old faiths or old ways of life to only be trapped again by a new set of values into which they put their hope for a better future.

This was a time for me to really, deeply live my life, experience my life and release whatever I really was.

Was this the real key to being happy? Zoomanity had gripped me for so long.

Was this all part of *my* great escape?

My Escape from Zoomanity

Have you done things in life when you look back and say, 'I always knew but never did anything about it?'

I know you're nodding your head in agreement as you think about those moments when you allowed things to carry on and on for what felt like forever until you snapped and took action.

I could share a million and one stories with you of tears and laughter. Maybe that's for another book.

What I do know is this. The lessons I have picked up along my life's travels created the man I am right now, today.

Lessons of strength, change, power, judgement, resistance, self-belief, family, love, standing firm, being resolute, and an awakening to the meaning of Zoomanity.

My life as a hairdresser, my life as a young boy, my life as an immigrant into England, my life as a minister, my life as a sales speaker, my life as a writer, poet, father, lover, and more, they have all flavoured this huge melting pot of cells that have become the person I am right now.

Being a minister served me in a good way despite the restrictions. Being a salon owner served me and all the other things I have done so far in my life served me in one way or another. Even the pain of divorce and humiliation bankruptcy – they all served me.

Yet my escape from Zoomanity was imminent.

Why? Because I always knew.

Part of me, the part you cannot see, the part that is never revealed but only to the person that is within, had been speaking to me for years.

Let's call this the Law of Humanity.

I was more than zooman, fully living the dream. Big home, big cars – everything I was told to chase and aim for, I had acquired.

The pains of life and the moments of magic were all there, yet the voice, that voice deep inside was speaking to me almost everyday.

I knew the way of zooman didn't work for me. Was it for me to sweat and toil endlessly to gather 'things' that had no real importance to me?

Life was supposed to be fun, alive, fresh, give me passion, and allow me to grow as a human being. That had all but vanished from my life. I wasn't growing, that's for sure, and when something isn't growing, it's dying. I was almost dead inside!

Yet my growth from a child had continually shown me and taught me things about life.

Moving from Scotland to England, seeing a man in space and walk on another planet, standing firm against school bullying as a child, standing firm against severe opposition as a minister of Jehovah's

Witnesses, divorce, bankruptcy, and so many other lessons life had all given me a gift. They were lessons that would shape, refine and return me to awaken from my Zoomanity and return to humanity.

But it would only be a gift if I could see the message in them. More and more the voice within was getting louder, the seeds of unhappiness were growing, the restrictions of self-placed boundaries were cracking and cracking faster and faster.

I had broken away from the Law of Zoomanity into the Law of Humanity and this was now changing fast into the Law of Re-creation. I wanted to re-create my life on my terms. I needed this more and more. I wanted a life based on reality, a new life that was born from my own escape from Zoomanity.

I wanted to make decisions for myself.

I wanted to create my own path.

I wanted to make my own mistakes and create my own glories.

I recall one day with my father as we walked along a beach in the Lake District in England. He revealed to me how if his life were a book, his last thirty years of life were blank pages. Dad told me how he wanted to do more, travel, create more, and experience life in its fullness.

I didn't want an empty book. I knew life's happiest people were those living their life on their terms. Salvation would only come from within, never from without or others.

Answering to a system and leading a lifestyle in the way of modern man, the zooman, no longer held me or fed me or was what I needed to wake up the way I wanted to wake.

For over two decades within my own family my opinions were suppressed. I was told to shut up and be quiet, stay in line and do as we all do.

I mean can you imagine how it felt being asked to sit at one side of a room and say nothing, offer no opinion on a better way of doing things while your in-laws moan and groan about their own lives and jobs? Some people love to be within their Zoomanity, they love the controls and the fixations and the drama of the endless ritual of conversation about how bad life is to them.

I recall a moment during one of these conversations where they all sat around the walnut oval table moaning about their jobs and lives. My ex-brother in law complained about how hard his job as a teacher was and all the trails and tribulations of the job were too much.

I made a simple suggestion: 'Why not change your career?'

They looked at me in utter horror, turned away and continued their zoomanic conversation that always led to the same conclusion, which was, 'It all works out fine when you retire'. Yet here was my ex-father-in-law at age seventy-four struggling and working on a farm, picking out weeds for extra cash, despite being a highly paid professional and saving all of his life.

Zoomanity's idea of the perfect life wasn't for me!

During that same period my intense and fundamentalist faith held me tight in its grip, telling me what way to walk, turn and think.

I had a fear of not going to the meetings but I also had a fear of going to them. Internally I felt torn in two. This habit of faith, the repeating beliefs, and not really asking questions anymore had me in denial and torment.

Peer pressure, family pressure, business pressure, home pressure, creating, building, buying more and more – it had become the perfect face of my own Zoomanity.

I had chosen this, of course. I'm blaming no one.

Wake up, go to work, come home, eat, and then watch endless TV until the cycle was repeated.

I hated TV running day after day after day. I hated the belief that the weekends were great but the weeks were to be passed as fast as possible only to meet another weekend.

I hated that everything was supposed to be the way it was because no one had dared to say otherwise. The adventure of life had become a monster.

I no longer wanted this. I no longer accepted it. A mortgage was the plan of mankind. A retirement plan was planned from almost my first day at work.

I can even remember guy named Roy Pacey from my first job as a gardener. Roy was an old grey-headed man whom I worked with at the age of sixteen as a landscape gardener.

My first week at work he asked me if I had planned a pension plan! Here's me, a sixteen-year-old punk rocker with red and green hair. The last thing I had on my mind was a pension plan. It was and is the way of Zoomanity. Train them early, condition them young, keep them in line.

My ex-father-in-law would go on and on and on about he had spent most of his life planning his pension. Sadly when it came to his pension time, in the UK we went through huge pension scandals. He, like a lot of others, found most of the savings he had invested for retirement over the years were suddenly of no value.

He was wiped out.

I'd had my life filled with these rules and follow-me ways of Zoomanity. Now was my time to push forward and grow.

This is the crisis point, the breaking point. You either go one way and release yourself or go the other way and follow the long line of zoomen into a life of nothing special.

The conditioning from my young days, my youth days, my adult days, and my older days never worked. It had failed me. The human deep inside me was always going to overrun the zooman.

I finally escaped. It was hard, never easy, and still has its waves, as you've seen and read. I made major decisions that were to re-shape my life and my family's lives forever.

It's said an early death can be brought about by certain events in a man's life: divorce, bankruptcy, death of my faith. I've survived them all so far and grown from them.

Loss of a twenty-year-old, fundamentalist, deeply engrained faith. Loss of my lifelong blood and non-blood family. Losing my lifetime family friends. Losing a five-bedroom luxury family home my children adored and I had carefully and lovingly built with my own hands. Having cars repossessed. A devastating, vicious, destructive, costly, bitter, long divorce. Death threats from members of my own family. The utter humiliation of bankruptcy and being known as a bankrupt within my business community. Health-related issues brought on by the endless stress and the final breakdown of my personal life.

My life had been un-picked, deconstructed, taken apart, piece by piece, memory by memory, moment by moment.

Yet the lessons were powerful for me.

A crisis in life reveals a lot of things. It also reveals who your family and friends really are. My brother Steve was a rock during this period and still is today. Never judging, just supporting. The rest vanished, judged and condemned. It taught me a lot about resistance to changes of any kind. Changes do take place, the inner human will always overcome the zooman if we allow the natural laws to run their course. When we resist each day only gets harder. I learned people are not who they say they are, they are stuck in a script of expectation, the Zoomanity repeatist beliefs and endless mind conditioning.

The loss of possessions taught me another huge amount about Zoomanity. Would I grieve the loss? No, not really. I learned despite having everything I had created myself in life, losing it despite the natural humiliation created a better human being. It gave me a sense of what life really is.

Recently I watched and listened to Gorbachev being interviewed. On being asked about his greatest moments in life, his triumphs, loves and failures his answer was simple.

Despite being a huge agent of change for mankind there was just one thing he wanted on his 80th birthday, it was his wife. She has died, he missed her and it was his life.

Life is never about things. Zoomanity had taught me, us that life is about collecting, amassing things for greater happiness.

I learned that life never was about them as I stood and watched the former people of my former life fight over tables, chairs and nothing in particular.

I also learned from bankruptcy, the shame and embarrassment was supposed to be there for me. To some extent it 3was yet I felt relieved that this was a closure being forced upon me by my first wife.

The whole episode a sad affair but made clear that there is a time to clean away the old to prepare for the new.

Near my parents home some time ago they were about to knock down a beautiful sixties building. It had been used on many TV shows for spy-esque type of things.

As I walked past I asked the men what was going on. They told me these old buildings can be fixed, repaired, patched and almost glued back together but there are times when it's best to demolish, remove and clear away everything to prepare the ground for something brand new that is designed to do exactly the right job.

Bankruptcy gave me a feeling of elation yet I also had that deep ingrained feeling of shame. Was I supposed to feel that way? People would say, "Bankrupt, how are you coping, how embarrassing, that's tough". The reality for me was very different. Cash had now become low in a list of priorities during my escape from Zoomanity.

Losing access to my children and finally losing the home I had built with my own bleeding fingers.

The kids, the manipulation, the pain, the grieving hurt. Zoomanity tells us to generate hate, anger and revenge during a divorce. It was a mess with my kids being manipulated within a sea of gossip and revenge. Today they are back they saw through it.

Life in Zoomanity is message loaded. We learn or repeat but as a real human we are smarter, much smarter. Yet the smartness has been covered, veneered by the age of conditioning and endless repeatisms from the ages of man.

Thank God, I had learned. I had escaped.

I took a choice. That choice had a result. It deconstructed my whole life. It was like a tsunami that flattened everything. I was left with a new blank canvas on which I could create what I wanted, how I wanted.

They were hard, depressing times and at the same time I felt a rejoicing because I had finally let go of all that was pinning my humanity firmly to the ground.

My greatest-ever escape had taken place – my own escape from Zoomanity. Life is message-packed. Your life and moments in your life changed you forever. The moments moulded you into who you are today. Yet we do not see most of those messages at the time. They are subtle parts of life that make deep, deep impressions. Looking back I see my own now. At the time I never did.

How about you? What changes have moulded your life?

The messages are strong. They shift, move and direct us to places we really don't see at the time. Yet the decisions ultimately lie with us. Do we decide or do we allow external forces to guide us from Zoomanity?

These are now exciting times packed with a new reality that life can be what I make it. What I was being taught through moments, messages and experiences over forty-eight years would help me create something new that would make me feel alive and awakened to the old world.

I no longer had to assume the outcome. I could plan and make things happen in a way that the restrictions of how things are meant to be would be removed forever. I now look forward to my next forty-eight years, my next life, and my next adventures.

It can be done. You can escape from your own self-inflicted Zoomanity, whatever it may be for you. For me the escape was complete. A zooman had been removed and the human had escaped from Zoomanity.

Awaken to Your Zoomanity

Do you feel like this?

Life is different from what you expected. You feel different about your job. In fact you hate it and can barely walk into the office anymore.

You are feeling overloaded with life itself, fed up, almost depressed, and have no one you feel you can talk it over with. Your relationship feels stale, dry, dusty. You have everything you need yet you feel like you have nothing. You've done all and more according to the blueprint, the layout, the path that each citizen of Zoomanity is supposed to live by.

Something inside of you, deep inside at a level or a feeling you've never had before, is feeling very strongly that this no longer fits your view of life and what life should be.

You're thinking about your life, your experiences and your lack of experiences. Is this it? Is this your life until death? Too much TV, too much work, too much bland tasteless life?

I know how you feel. Don't worry, you are starting to wake up and become aware of the humanity within trying to break free.

You now ask questions daily.

Is there more to life than this?

Does God or something more exist?

Will the universe really deliver what I ask?

Do I have to do this until I die?

Is this it?

Why do I have to live according to the rules of others?

Can changes in my life be made?

Is it too late for you to change?

The universe, God, politicians, Zoomanity, *you*…

Who's in charge of your life? Are you asleep or awake? Do you question everything? You are told not to but why is it you are told not to? Who said you shouldn't? Did the dream work out? Do you love your job? Was university worth it? Was the overtime worth it?

It feels like a million questions we are told *not* to ask but slowly you are starting to awaken to the created environment around you.

Zoomanity has held you in fear, caged, restricted, now you are awakening.

It's begun!

We of course create our own life experiences as far as we can and as much as freedom allows, but that raises another question: how much freedom do we truly have?

Ultimately we all die. Seventy, eighty, maybe ninety or more years we have to fill.

Create a book of your life. When its read will it have hearts pulsating or have hearts and minds saying, 'Was that it?'

You want to feel the need to leave a good, strong history for your family, kids or friends.

The reality is we have to fill the bit from birth to death.

How well are you doing that? If it were literally a book, would you be happy with what you read?

Life should be, and has to be, about adventure, passion, experience, love, life, living, pain, tears and almost every other experience we can think about.

How many adventures can you write about? How many adventures can you share with your family and your own kids?

The purpose of Zoomanity is control. Control led through fear. Fear of the unknown of an impending something that never really arrives.

When the battle for the mind is won, you are under the control of Zoomanity. When under its control you are locked in tight until death.

You become a number in a bigger picture, used and abused. To order – to buy – click here and do what you are told. Stay in line, ask no questions!

Zoomanity gives you what it has trained you to believe you need. The happier you are, the more you buy. You have become a passive zooman. The cycle is set in stone until you break out!

Go back to the beginning. You are born.

As you develop and grow you are taught and trained. The training could be religious, it could be atheist, it could be agnostic, it could be anything, but the reality is that training takes place from the day we arrive.

The child is predetermined to follow the training of those the child feels safe with. Parents, teachers, (even creepy teachers) and other people in authority.

Then you begin to grow, develop, and start on your own life path. Decisions are made based on what you know. Most of the time what you know is what you have been taught or shared from others.

The 'others' include family, media, newspapers, respected leaders, politicians, religious teachers – in fact all of those in place to guide and share with you their thoughts on a better life.

The problem is, of course, that you are not them and they are not you.

Zoomanity knows that. Nothing is in place by accident. It's all there for a reason. That reason is to keep you in place, like the large elephant in the zoo, passive and controlled.

Your life continues, you grow, mature, age and at some point death will arrive.

How was it for you? How was your life? Did the repeatist patterns of others serve you and serve you well?

Who gave them what they teach us? Do they know the origin of the teachings?

Most are repeatists in a sleeping pattern as far as deeper awakened thoughts go. How do we know?

Well, what is a repeatist? A repeatist creates the zooman with their repeated thoughts.

Very simple: they repeat what they have been told and rarely question the ideal or thought behind it. They simply accept what they have been told as fact!

I think a very good example of repeatism comes from the *theory* of evolution. The fact is that it is a theory, not a proven fact. Yet for decade it has been taught as a fact.

Now I am not saying I agree or disagree but the reality is we have this theory based on repeatism taught to humanity from a very young age. Does that thought provoke you? I hope so. It was meant to create a thought explosion in your mind.

There are a million cases on both a tiny scale and a global scale where Zoomanity has been wrong. Sometimes it takes just a magical moment in time to make us wake up and become aware of that.

People like Ghandi transformed the world with their new way of thinking. Yet it actually isn't always new at all. Ghandi simply dug a little deeper, returned to humanity, and asked questions. 'Was it right for another man to treat and other so badly because of his skin and caste?' It clearly was never the original way of man so where had it come from?

Ghandi's and others' ways of thinking were just a very real human way based on love and the covered feelings of man. If we love each other as a human race, skin, language, and denomination have no real meaning over love.

Ghandi questioned what had been repeated to him.

It takes me back a little to when I was a minister. Despite the fact I studied and studied hard there were also lots of things I accepted as they were told to me. The things that were told to me I would knock on peoples' doors and share those messages with the house-holders.

But today I question that and I questioned it as I drifted away. I had faith; of course it was right – but was it? I was repeating to others the best way of doing things yet it had started to *not* feel the best way for me to do things.

Have you done that? Done things, repeated things without questioning? This is the trait of the zooman. This is what makes the perfect zooman. Zoomanity wants you to question nothing.

And that brings us back to modern day Zoomanity.

Let's think about this in your life context. Now I am not saying what you are about to read is your life, of course; I am simply saying what I am writing has implications that could affect your life and awaken you to another way of looking at your own life.

The basic intention of any man is to do better or do his best to be as happy as possible. He is fed an endless procession of 'must have more of everything and anything.' This is the consumer society created by the repeatists – the upholders (or profit makers) of Zoomanity.

Have you seen and felt this in your life so far?

And on the thought of consumption or consuming, it's interesting to me that we think of consumers as people who buy and destroy through their greed. This is where Zoomanity has been clever because a little thought shows it goes way beyond that. The consumer also consumes (eats, devours) into himself/herself information at a faster rate than ever before. People wake almost with a smart phone in their hands, check email, text, social media and maybe the news before they leave their place of rest in the morning.

This consumption of information feeds our very being, it alters the way think and see, and twists, diverts and tugs at even our deepest emotions. What we consume into our body or minds is clearly what we become!

My mum knows about the flu months before she gets flu.

She will say to me, 'Have you heard about this new flu?'

I reply, 'No mum I haven't.'

Mum then says, 'It's coming and it's going to be bad.'

As the weeks go by mum keeps asking about the flu and saying how it is racing towards me like a heat seeking missile and how I will get it.

Six weeks later, guess what? Mum has the flu.

She'll call me with that real sorry voice and say, 'You never guess what – I got that flu.'

'Really, mum,' I will reply.

'You'll be next,' she tells me.

Interesting. What we continually feed our minds, we become. This is the *attraction factor* in action.

How about you, do you ever question what you consume? We are all of course what we eat, mentally and physically.

I have a pal who is clearly very overweight. He eats pizza, burgers and almost any kind of junk food. He drinks more cola than anyone I know. In fact he has a bottle in his hand all of the time.

Every time we meet he tells me I am looking fit and healthy. He then says the same thing he always says: 'I'd love to get fitter and healthier and lose some weight.'

Why does he say that when the answer is clear on how he got to where he is right now?

Is he questioning or repeating?

The question is, what do you feed your mind and your body?

Zoomanity wants you to question *nothing*. It wants you to be controlled without you feeling you are being controlled.

Have you begun to ask questions, to question almost everything?

You are starting to wake up. Your escape from Zoomanity has begun. Almost nothing will now stop it.

Average John, Average Zooman

John is John, just average guy John.

He lives his life exactly as he is told or others have repeated to him, the Zoomanity way.

He works hard at school as he is told he should. The teacher tells him if he doesn't get his results his life will come to nothing. Some kids in the class don't like to work. John believes they will come to nothing and he will be a success with a happier life than them.

He gets his almost perfect grades, and now he is on his way to a better stronger more guaranteed future. John accepts, believes and questions nothing.

'Work hard, John,' they keep telling him, 'And you'll be something or someone at some point in your life.'

John of course wants what everybody else wants. Big house, detached, no neighbours, with a big driveway with brand new BMWs or other prestige cars on his driveway. Why not? It's the dream right?

Who set the dream?

John finally leaves university with his degree in political history. Now he also has a student loan to contend with.

No matter, John will have to simply get an even better job so he can also cover his student loan. His debt from his university days is at £25,500.

John gets on the 'ladder' of life (interesting term don't you think – the ladder – yet where does the climb take us to, where we expect?).

Gets a decent job. Gets his first house. Adding cash into his bank account and even has enough to pay for his student debts.

His parents and grandparents are proud of John, he's doing really well and he knows it. His friends are envious.

John questions nothing, he does as he is told, he listens to the repeatists, he's unaware of his ongoing conditioning and is committed to the almost invisible ways of Zoomanity.

John gets older. Gathers more, gains more, increases his debts for a better life. He might have debts but he feels the two weeks a year holiday is good compensation for his hard work.

In fact when he comes home from his favourite holiday place in Spain, John and his wife talk about it for the next twelve months until they go again.

John's patterns are now set in stone.

He loves the weekends but dreads Monday morning. He doesn't like Tuesdays either. In fact he has begun to hate almost all his days at work.

When asked how was his weekend his replies are always the same: 'Great, can't wait until the week is over.'

John's weeks are now revolving around his weekends.

Think about John here for a second.

He now hates five days a week and enjoys just two of them. Week after week, month after month, he wishes those five days would pass. Which means that over fifty working years, John is wishing away 13,000 days of his life. Days he wishes would end.

His life now revolves around:

Holidays

Bank holidays
Christmas
Easter
New things
New cars
Gathering more
Working harder.

This carries on for the next twenty years.

John has just reached forty. His two kids are growing fast. His wife is happy, his parents are proud, but there is a problem.

John is not only older but working harder than ever. Each month he has to work even harder than ever to pay mortgage, car loans, student debt, credit cards, and multiple other outstanding small loans. Despite the fact he has his wages of £75,000 or more he never feels like there will be enough to pay everything.

And of course what about holidays, Christmas, paying for his kids' education, buying more stuff to replace older stuff and looking after his home that needs to be maintained?

One day he wakes up. He does not want to go to work. As John is walking from the train to his city office he stops dead in his tracks and just stares forward. His leather briefcase in his left hand starts to slowly slip from his fingers. Sweat pours from his forehead. His shirt feels damp, sticky and tight around his neck. His grey suit feels blacker than black, his skin is pale apart from the dark rings that hang so heavy beneath his aged, wrinkled, sagging eyes.

'What am I doing here?'

'I can't do this.'

'It's not what I'd hoped for.'

'My life is more important than this.'

'I have had enough.'

John snaps. This is his moment of change. He is starting to awaken. Awaken to what? Awaken to the fact that the life he has been living so far is getting harder and harder, not easier and easier as he was promised it would be as a young college graduate.

He accepted everything he had been told from the media, from his family, from his friends, magazines, and from movies that the pursuit of consumption would give him a life to be envied and desired. They repeated, he accepted. He questioned nothing.

Now he's questioning everything. It wasn't true anymore for him. He is now facing his worst fears in the face.

If he drops out from what he is supposed to be, the expectation, everything will become a mess. John has calculated to retire with everything paid off he will be sixty-eight years old and not have enough cash in the bank to even pay for one holiday a year.

Now John is looking at his life with new eyes. This is his time to stop dead and re-think how he lives his life.

Or is it?

What will others think?

What will his wife say?

What will his family say?

Can he actually make changes?

Will he make the changes needed to re-create his Happiness, or should he live and die with regrets?

One John thing knows for sure: he can't carry on the way he is carrying on.

John has hit his moment. His own deep, embedded law of humanity is starting to kick in, awaken and come to the surface and it's coming fast like a tsunami. Not a thing will stop it, apart from John himself.

John talks to his wife but she isn't interested in listening to him. She wants more furniture for the house, more gathering, more gain, more significance in the town they live.

John talks to his friends. They tell him it'll pass, get a grip, it's the normal way, and the conversation changes.

The only person John can now speak to is John. It's his decision and his decision only.

Will John escape from his Zoomanity, his cage, his restrictions, his controls from a life of conditioning and repeating?

This is the point when a life can only go one of two ways.

There are laws within all of us. These laws most of Zoomanity will brush away as rubbish or weird thinking.

The law of the awakening

This is where a moment takes place and we awaken from where we are right now.

The law of humanity

This is a law deep within where the human being can no longer be repressed by Zoomanity and needs to – *must* – break out and remove the veneers of conditioning and time.

The law of deliberate re-creation

This is where the new free human will deliberately recreate his or her life despite the massive pains or hardships they will endure during this time.

You cannot see these laws. You can feel them. And you have the choice between two paths:

One: Listen to the zooman and carry on, miserable and trapped, until you are sixty-eight, broke, and retired.

Two: Make massive changes now before its too late.

Zoomanity hates those who question anything. How about you?

Are you willing to face fears of your own and question everything?

Your Early Life

Did you get the message that was sent to you?

What message?

Think back, back a long way, and look into your book and your life as an early zooman. What were you taught by your parents? How did they teach you? Was their lesson something they do that you now always do?

Think back to a moment that has never left you. You are between the ages of four to six years.

Something was about to take place in your young life that you never forgot.

OK, take ten seconds to think about it.

Have you got it?

So now take that moment and build a picture around it. Where were you, how old were you, and how did it affect you?

Did you get the message?

Repeat this process and look back over the years between four and sixteen. List the moments that left a deep stamp on you. Reflect on those moments and look at the message.

The message is the part of the event that you didn't see at the time but when you look back and really look over the whole picture you will see there was a message in that event for you.

Like in my early years when my parents moved from Scotland to England. As a child it was an adventure but looking back the message really was that if it isn't working there are times in your life you have to take drastic action. My parents saw that if they remained the same their life could no longer continue as they were hoping.

They took an almost huge leap of faith and moved from one country to the other. It may seem like nothing these days but in 1969 it was a huge deal and certainly *not* what our family and friends approved of. In fact my parents were always seen as snobs and outcasts for making such a huge move.

Yet the move was their escape from Zoomanity and its chains at that time. But as a child I only saw the adventure, not the message.

How about you? Can you now read the message in the actions of moments of the past that you have just given some thought to?

Is Zoomanity holding you so tight that you can see it but fear is stopping you from looking at it in a way that you know if you go too deep you will have to make a change?

You are starting to become aware you are on the edge of your moment of change.

It is coming – or not. The choice is yours!

Your Young Life in Zoomanity

Life is littered with messages for you. Let's move forward to the young man or woman you are now. Can you look back and think back?

When I was seventeen my mum took me on a driving lesson. Mum and my sister were both training to be state registered nurses (SRNs).

As we drove back to my house in our yellow Vauxhall cavalier we drove over a small humpback bridge. As we came over the other side I noticed right away an old woman lying on the street. Next to her was an old man leaning on a walking stick looking shocked and staring at her. The woman was his wife.

They looked to be around eighty-something in years. I said to mum we must stop. Mum and my sister said even though they were both trainee nurses they could not by law help the old lady and use or give medical attention in case they hurt or even killed her.

It was clear the old woman would die or was dying or even dead anyway.

Despite what mum said, I slammed on the brakes and jumped out of the car. The old man had tears streaming down his face. Mum realised she could not just leave the lady despite the law.

Between my mother and sister they quickly removed her false teeth and threw them on the pavement, removed her long coat, ripped open her blouse to fully expose her skin and old flesh. Mum gave her mouth to mouth as my sister hit hard and harder on the chest to try and kick-start her heart.

It was too late. The old lady had died. The ambulance arrived and took away the body of the old woman. Her old husband climbed into the back of the ambulance to take her to the morgue and then to her burial.

We went home. I went into my bedroom and cried for hours. Mum couldn't console me. I had just seen an undignified death, the end of an old life before my eyes. Even today I see clearer than ever the message in that moment.

Zoomanity had created an outrageous rule that trainee nurses could not assist someone who urgently needed their help.

But in the end the law of humanity over-rode the rules of Zoomanity.

A split-second of questioning. Who created the rule and was it going to benefit this dying woman? I learnt that humanity must take first place.

I also saw and learnt the fragility of a human life. Not knowing what was about to take place, the woman awoke in the morning and went to the shops with her husband. That evening he returned to their home alone to make plans for the burial of his wife.

The message is clear. Life is fragile. What do we – what do I – do with my time? That moment has never left me.

How about you? What are you doing with your time?

Can you go back in time once more and take out another moment from your young life? Can you hit the replay button in your mind and watch it play again? Is it too painful for you? Yet if you re-run the moment the lesson will be huge. Your parents' painful divorce. Having to leave your family home and watch the breakdown and destruction of your family life.

I spoke to a neighbour. The guy and his wife did not discuss their relationship – or to be more blunt, sex. After all, according to Zoomanity sex is not to be talked about. He had gone off sex. In fact they had not had a sexual relationship with each other for over six months.

One day she got home before him. As he walked in she sat at the kitchen table, almost grey with tears in her eyes.

'Steve, I have had sex with another man, I am truly sorry, I wish it had not happened, please forgive me, I will make it up to you.'

Steve replies with one word: 'Why?'

She replies, 'It's been six months. I just wanted to feel loved and held again by my man, but you rejected me.'

How do you think Steve reacted?

I know you'll have the reply but lets re-phrase the question.

How do you think Steve was *expected* to react?

And if he was expected to react this way, why?

His reaction was rage, temper, and infuriation to the point he destroyed her belongings and threw her out.

Was the problem that she had slept with another man or was her sleeping with another man the symptom of something much bigger?

Zoomanity has the zooman trained to act and react in certain ways to certain situations. Steve's reaction was classic textbook zooman.

Why? Steve refused to question his own behaviour for the past six months. In fact he questioned nothing.

Is this a trait of Zoomanity?

Steve had his beautiful wife in front of his eyes daily but he refused to unplug himself from TV, media, work and a million other distractions.

Has Zoomanity restricted you in a way where the past is the past and should never be re-visited? Why?

Think about it. Think deeply about your life right now. The path, the events, the moments, the places you have been to and walked through in your life.

Did you get the messages that were left for you?

Steve will look back at some point in his life and see the message from his divorce. The message was that it was about him, not her at the time. It might even be about both of them. Either way there was a lot to learn from his zoomanic approach to the woman who was then his wife. It was predictable and textbook.

Zoomanity says question nothing. Humanity has created you to be an inquisitive creature filled with adventure and experience. To do that you must question everything.

Will you?

Shaping of the Zooman

You're getting older. How does it feel?

Do you awaken each day with excitement and passion for life? Do you have zeal and zest for living the life you truly desire?

Or did you awaken this morning dreading the thought of going to work on the train, tube, bus, car or even a short flight into the city?

Are the weekends – *two days a week* – more important to you that the other five days? If you said yes, Zoomanity has you in its grip and its all part of the plan!

Let me take you back to when I bought my first house. In England at that time we had something known as an endowment mortgage.

Very simply this meant that if we would get a huge lump of cash as a down payment, at the end of the mortgage period of twenty-five years we could own our home.

As a young man I had never bought a house. I knew nothing about buying a house, yet I had been told time and time again that I would have to buy a house. (It's a sin of Zoomanity that we don't teach kids simple economics of buying a house.)

So of course I went into the adviser's at my bank and she sold (pushed on me) me this endowment concept I had no idea about, called an endowment policy. I trusted them as *the* experts. After all I was simply a hairdresser in those days!

To cut a long story short, the endowment system failed and after investing cash into it for fifteen years my policies became worthless. A £7,000 investment was worth less than a £1,000.

Think about this, I was told time and time again that I *must* have endowments.

Who told them to tell me that I should do that? Who is telling you? Where does this stuff come from originally?

It'll have origins with the cash maker: create a new cash product, get in fast, sell it to everyone, and the theory should work. If it doesn't do you think *they* will suffer or will *you*?

Look what happened to global banking in 2009. Think of all those people that lost hundreds, thousands, and even millions of pounds.

Did the bankers suffer? Did they even lose their jobs? In most cases the answer is there for anyone to read: no they did not.

They were supported and bailed out by national governments. Using whose money? Yes – your cash, your money, your taxes.

In other words you lost out twice if you lost money during that period.

So if you lost a truck load of cash you were then expected to accept that you would lose it again by bailing out the banks, allowing them to use your taxes to bail out the guys you were told listen and follow.

Can you see what the zoo keepers do here? Think this over. Who is in control – you or the zoo keepers (governments and authorities)?

Are you seeing your life in the story of Zoomanity?

Lets go back in time again into your life.

Can you pinpoint a moment where the financial system created by Zoomanity signed you up, locked you in, and tied you down?

The financial ways of Zoomanity, I have to admit, have been a past downfall of mine. Making plenty but spending plenty more.

Why do we never teach the reality of economics to our children? Maybe if Zoomanity did that they would lose huge amounts of profits, profiteering on our lack of experience and our immaturity.

Is your life marred with cash problems? Weird, though, because maybe you earn more than most people you know but you are always broke. Maybe you cannot break through the earnings level to where you want to be. Maybe earning is just something you have told yourself you are just not good at?

Have you told yourself those things because that is what is repeated to you?

'It's OK for him, he's got cash.'

'It's easy for them – they have the cash to do it.'

Do you say things like that about others or are we really saying that about others to justify our own financial 'position?

Zoomanity hates you to be financially independent. It hates you to be smart about money. Even the rich find it hard to be rich within the rules of Zoomanity.

I met a guy who was making over twenty-five million a year. He drove Rolls Royces, lived in penthouses, and wore the finest, most expensive clothing.

Today he is broke.

Why?

He was a working-class man who learnt how to make huge amounts as an entrepreneur.

His downfall was very simple.

Although he earns twenty-five million a year, he could easily spend 26, 27, 28, or 30 million or more. His whole life was on lease, homes, cars, watches, rings, clothing – the whole caboodle. He couldn't keep up with the payments. Busted again.

The funny thing about this guy is that he's gone bust four times now. He repeats the same old patterns time and time again.

The reality is that unless you control your life at a very personal level, you make and take decisions based on firm research and proven (or as proven as they can be) facts then you will always be a zooman trapped inside Zoomanity.

I learned that the only person responsible for my cash was *me*, not the bankers. They are there to do one thing only – to make a profit!

How about you and your young adult life? Has it turned out as expected? Can you look back over time and pinpoint maybe a moment when finances became hard, tough, and maybe unreachable?

Was it a job or career that went wrong? An investment where you lost? A banking crisis? A costly divorce? A bankruptcy?

Was there something that took place in your life that when looking back there was a message for you?

Now you are awakening, becoming more aware, and more conscious. Are you seeing the message for what it really was?

You didn't see it then but you see it now. Something that happened to mum and dad or to one of them.

As my kids look back on my bankruptcy I could share lessons with them now, but I know they simply wouldn't get it.

The lessons for myself as a man were huge.

Humiliation, collapse of business, no wealth, and control being given to the authorities of my finances so they (Zoomanity) could put me back on track again.

I love the old 1973 movie called *Westworld* starring the actor Yul Brynner (look it up – fantastic movie). The android goes crazy, loses control, and wants to destroy everything. Almost a visionary movie for future times.

Zoomanity is always waiting in the wings for you to build and repair you according to their presets and repeatist patterns.

They want to condition, refine, and repair you to run smoothly.

Get born, grow, condition, develop, tie in to the dream, retire, and die.

It's really very simple for them.

The more control they have at the level of a single human the more they control you, the man. The more individuals they control the more they control humanity. The control of humanity becomes Zoomanity.

Lets go back to the question. Did you see the messages from your own past? Did you pinpoint the moment when it all went horribly wrong for you or something happened in your life, a moment an event that changed you?

The messages are never that clear but they are there in you. Take time, dig deep, and go back.

You are veneered in the laws of Zoomanity. Make no mistake – if you are reading this book the laws of humanity for you are getting closer and closer.

Just on that note I want to share this.

Every important decision that I have allowed others to make for me in my life has always backfired. Cash, relationships, business – who decides for you, your own humanity or the controls of Zoomanity?

You're Now in the Thick of Zoomanity

A realisation takes an almost immeasurable moment in time. It's a split second when we become aware of something. We're rarely sure quite what that something is but we know something isn't quite right.

Let's look at you.

Where is your life right now as you read this book?

Broke?

Divorced?

In drama?

In a story?

Bored senseless?

Job slave?

Trapped by cash?

On TV sometime ago, I watched (don't tell anyone ;-) *X-Factor*, a TV talent show for the almost talentless. A lady came on to the stage from Ireland, she was forty-nine years old I think. She then had to share a little about her life.

She told how many years ago she had been badly maimed in a car bomb. She told how this moment in her life had defined her life until this point and had actually destroyed her life.

She had children and a good husband yet she still would say this event destroyed her whole life.

They asked what winning the show would mean to her?

She told them it would change her life and make it worth living.

She didn't win the show.

But I wondered.

Was she behaving the way Zoomanity likes us or conditions us to behave? Was the reality that her life was pretty good, her husband and kids were great, and she looked well and healthy? And yet when we go through a drama of any kind it can define and shape us forever.

I'm not underestimating her pain and trauma, but she was clearly an example of that. She told the story because that was what she was supposed to do – tell the story. She believed that it had destroyed her life and yet the reality may be was it had affected her life but not destroyed her life.

Was she simply acting out a role that would be played time and time again until her life ceased to be?

At the same time I read an interview with a young man in a magazine. He had lost both his legs in war. He shared how it had transformed his life for the *better*. He had even climbed Everest with no legs.

How about you? Have you experienced an event that has shaped you this way? It was so dramatic, traumatic that it's just there and won't go away?

Zoomanity likes everyone to play the role and live the script. Moments – your life is made up of moments, that's all. They can define you for all time in a negative way if you allow them to. They can define you in a positive way for change and more change. Has that happened to you? Have you been fooled by Zoomanity into playing the role, when actually the roles usually create more destruction?

I have personally been through a divorce. It's a terrible, painful destructive act that leaves a deep scar on the people involved.

But it is also this: A divorce is an argument that is never settled. It is left to settle and fester as the roles are played out as defined by Zoomanity.

Why?

Did Zoomanity teach you about relationships? Did it teach you that everything will work out fine but when it goes wrong you play out a role? Did it teach you nothing and you are simply trying to get your way through life?

As a fully grown captive within Zoomanity, you are held in certain fears. Yet fears are just thoughts of an expectation of what may take place. The fears can be overcome when we look back at how we were moulded, whey we were moulded that way, and how we have grown and developed.

I have a friend who has never spoken to her father since her parents' divorce forty-one years ago. She is a reclusive, shy, bitter character. She says her father destroyed her life. I have another friend who not only went through the divorce of his parents but watched his Mother remarry five times and get divorced another five times, and then finally he went through his own divorce. He believes these experiences have made him a strong, powerful man who can help others grow and believe in their own potential.

Can you see the difference?

Zoomanity is asking you to play the role all the time. Are you playing along as expected?

The career man.

The wealth collector.

The *Truman Show*-style family man.

More cars.

More holidays.

Question everything!

Your life so far has created what you are today for good or for bad. Yet the fact is you are where you are and what you are by choice. The repeatism and condition of Zoomanity forces you into a role and most of us play the roles.

Zoomanity has been created to suppress and control your life. What is your personal Zoomanity? Do you know?

It's worth repeating that Zoomanity was created for a reason. That reason is to make sure everything goes according to plan. Whose plans? The plans of those who control mankind.

It goes beyond the family, beyond the career, beyond most things.

As I write this there's an example taking place of a zooman in full bloom in the Asana Tea House here in California.

To my left there are four people sitting around a table. Three are ladies; two are maybe in their sixties and one, who is around twenty-five, hasn't spoken. A guy that I would guess is around fifty but looks more like sixty-five is the one dominating the conversation.

For the past forty-five minutes, during every topic of conversation that has risen he has quickly jumped in feet first and added a negative slant to everything. The conversation keeps coming back to 'there are no jobs.' He is unemployed and all the rich are taking it away from him personally. He is bitter. His face has the lines of hard done to written all over it. He is bitter and in denial of his reality.

He feels the rich should be stripped and people like him should be given handouts to help him and improve his life. He once worked in Silicon Valley for Abode, he says, and he was made unemployed five years ago. He hates them. He sounds like he hates everyone and is going on and on about how Adobe needed him.

Now I'm not judging this guy or the conversation; I am simply observing how mind thoughts are placed. What he is saying is a mind game and a mind trap from Zoomanity. The negative thoughts are placed from quite a young age through media, conversation, TV shows, movies, books, magazines, governments, and so on.

This in itself creates a deeper inner fear within the zooman. When the zooman is in fear he looks to another to direct, guide and protect him.

The unemployed guy appears to have surrendered to the idea of not having any hope at all. He wants a job (or does he?) but he believes a job is not possible. We know that simply isn't true; work and jobs and creating cash are always possible.

He talks non-stop about recession, depression and lost hope. Is that what he is attracting into his life? It looks that way and sounds that way.

Think about it.

He experiences life in twenty-four-hour chunks like you and me. His life is option-based yet his options are based around repeatist patterns. He is saying what the media have been pummelling endlessly into him since he was a child. He is repeating what his parents used to say, what his work mates used to say, and what his friends used to say.

Is he questioning anything? Sure he is – he's questioning everything except his own behaviour.

Is this your moment? Are you wakening up now, last week, last month, last year?

Is it time for you to break out, smash the fence, create and re-generate your own life and your own escape from Zoomanity?

Zoomanity, the Cult of the Zooman, and the Great Escape

The cult.

It sounds dark and ominous, like brain control and more, but actually a quick check on the word makes it clear.

The word first appears in early 1600 and comes from another word which basically means to cultivate.

Are you a member of the Zoomanity?

Maybe you said no, but let's think about this because Zoomanity is the world's biggest and most subliminal cult.

Almost no one knows of its existence.

Go into any city early in the morning and observe. Go to any place the masses flock to and observe.

Do you see masses of people almost like robots doing the same thing, or do you see many individuals?

Walking, heading out, going to.

Most do as they are told, question nothing, and follow the cult of Zoomanity. Do you think you have done that in your life? Have you done the expected and it hasn't turned out as you wanted?

Zoomanity are your silent masters. Zoomanity cultivates you, me, and everyone to become adherents to the ways expected or the ways of conformity or the ways they have outlined, created, and programmed as best for you.

Now I'm *not* inciting anarchy or such like behaviour; of course I am simply saying for you to escape from Zoomanity you need to be aware and be awake to this kind of thinking – or should we say *non*-thinking.

Zoomanity always places happiness into the future, and rarely in the now, in the moment. It says you can be happy now, but not for too long. True lasting happiness is coming with the next thing sometime in the future.

Now lets think about that. If happiness is placed in the future that means we can never really truly be happy, can we?

Does the future ever arrive? Yes and no. Think about this. Here is how Zoomanity set us up.

We look forward to:

Weekends.

Holidays.

Birthdays.

Gifts.

New home.

New car.

New anything.

New government.

The list becomes endless but the fact is Zoomanity is designed to hold you *now*, to keep you fixed and held firmly in its tight grip.

Do you feel trapped, unable to decide anymore, and do you simply allow your life to go with the flow of what is expected? Yet deep down, deep inside you feel unhappy, bitter, sad and struggling to keep going?

Your breakout has begun!

Here's an interesting thought I have thought about on many occasions.

Earlier, I talked about mid-life crisis.

A phrase, a word, a condition – I'm not sure. Here is what I *am* sure about: a crisis is usually a thing that is a symptom of a far greater problem.

I believe that those who have a mid-life crisis are showing the peak symptoms of being victims of Zoomanity. The pressure to endlessly conform, stay in line, to be part of what is expected becomes too much, and at some point the pressure blows.

Those are the ones who get to a point in their lives and are about to either awaken or fall into a deep endless sleep that they may never recover from.

Such a person is a cliché of Zoomanity.

What do you think?

Could this person get a job? People will pay cash for almost anything.

Wash the car.

Cut the grass.

Build me something.

Move the trash.

Odd-job man.

And just about anything.

Now I know for some things we need extra skills but there are a lot of things that need no skills in particular.

Yet the mind has been told that we cannot think outside our own range of skills. Is that a fact or is that a mind-myth created and fed to us by Zoomanity?

The guy at the tea house was a software engineer. But he could change his skills and change his life. Zoomanity has told him otherwise. His identity is wrapped up with his skill set and he has no idea how to break out from that identity. As far as he is concerned his is and will always be a software engineer.

So here is what takes place. People build their own story of what is and what isn't. People will say 'I do or I don't like that,' when the reality is they have never tried it and their beliefs are usually passed on from another person.

They are usually repeating what they have heard, what they have been told, or what they have read. Most of these opinions – and that's what they are – are they valid or not? That's for you to decide, but here's what I do know: to have a valid opinion or thought on anything we really have had to try and experience those things, right?

I mean would you tell your friend not to buy a Volvo if you knew nothing about Volvos? Maybe you would, because that is the kind of thing people do.

Again (not to go on), whenever people discover I was a minister of Jehovah's Witness they *always* and without fail offer an opinion.

Now what usually takes place when people find this out is that they tell me something about this faith of which I was a member for twenty years.

What they tell me almost 100% of the time is wrong.

They tell me things I have heard more than once yet they tell me with total conviction that it is a fact.

I ask them this: 'Have you studied this faith as an impartial observer?'

They always say 'no.' There isn't a lot to say after that.

I know, as I have already studied this faith for over twenty years, so of course I know the truth of what they believe.

However, this goes to show one thing. How fiction can be seen and perceived as a fact. True? This is a speciality of Zoomanity.

How many times have you personally encountered this?

Let me take you back to the software engineer guy at the tea house. Yes, he is still talking. The young girl is frozen with fear. The guy has repeated time and time again that she is part of a lost generation that will never have any hope (yes, he has said that time again). The girl has fired back and told him she has hope and she will be successful creating her position on the local radio station she is working with.

Her mind is young and fresh. His mind has been cluttered, tamed, harnessed, and boxed by Zoomanity. He won't change and he doesn't want to. She can still create her own escape – she just has to be aware of what Zoomanity is and how it works. He could of course wake up, but Zoomanity has taught him that his life is over!

Lessons From Silicon Zoomanity

There are lessons here, huge ones.

Do we believe everything we hear or read and repeat it as a fact? That's exactly what Zoomanity wants from you. To hold you down and force you into repeating so-called facts. This creates a mind that is boxed in with a belief that nothing can change and things will always be as they are, when the reality is most of the facts that we are told are *not* facts.

How about you and your life? Do you need change? Do you want change? Can you change? Are you in fear of change?

You will hit a point when you want to either recreate your life or simply wait around for death.

All of us have choices – but do we make them ourselves or allow others to do so?

Hiding from Zoomanity

Is it possible to hide away and avoid Zoomanity? Well yes and no, but I want to share something I have seen time and time again during my travels around the planet.

As I type here in Santa Cruz California (a place I absolutely adore) I am amongst some of those who have made a huge effort to hide away in a small corner of the world from the pressures and rules of Zoomanity.

Let me give you an example.

Let's take a place like Santa Cruz where I am right now. People come literally from all over the USA to be here. They love it and adore it. It's warm, artistic, creative and cheap to live.

Yes, sure it has to stick to the laws of the state of California, yet at the same time it does almost its own thing. Santa Cruz is a true remnant of the hippie movement, that 1960s movement that self-destructed and eventually put just more politicians into power.

Amongst the great things (and there are a million things that are incredible about Santa Cruz), what was left over is a crass version of peace and love that has been absorbed in drugs and a lack of self worth.

Paul is from a broken home in the Midwest. He hates not only his life but he wants to fight and beat Zoomanity. Paul's buddy tells him about a place called Santa Cruz. It's good for several reasons. You can live on the streets pretty successfully if you need to. The rules here are pretty laid back and drugs are cheap and freely used. But here's the big thing: it has a community that is tight and will always look after its own.

Just the other day I spoke to a homeless guy that by his own admission was totally wasted with drugs and drink. He was sober when we spoke. I asked him about his lifestyle on the streets and I can tell you he was very direct in a lot of what he told me.

I asked him why he hasn't managed to get out from Santa Cruz. His answer was very simple: the community supported him and that kept him in. He has tried to get out but now feels he has a total reliance on the community that he has lived in for the past few years.

So Paul arrives in Santa Cruz. He has nothing but believes this is the best way to hide out from Zoomanity.

Unfortunately for Paul, this is going to be an even bigger lockdown than the place he has come from. Why? The community will love and adore Paul and they will support him with what they can, but the sad reality is they will want Paul to share the life they are already living. This simply means that Paul, once he's in, will struggle to get out.

The community also has rules. Paul has to share what he owns and that's not a lot. He won't pay taxes but he has to pay for drugs. He won't have to work but he will have to beg on the streets. More Zoomanity.

This self-imposed nirvanic state is fool's gold. Most people like Paul don't realise it until it's far too late and life is overtaken by a drug-induced stupor.

These kinds of towns appear to attract the absolute genius minds of Zoomanity and you can see it and feel it. As I walk along the streets around here the musicianship from the street performers is pretty incredible. Yet these are the places that seem to offer an escape from Zoomanity when in fact they are another version, a cloaked version of Zoomanity.

Zoomanity doesn't care. It wants control – control of you and no more. The more humankind is controlled the more gain for Zoomanity. Passive peaceful humans transformed into clone-like humans.

Hippies grow up and become part of the system. Punks grow up and become part of the system. Skaters grow up and become part of the system.

They all mostly do.

Those that don't seem to be controlled take an extreme path of excess within their own community. Yet the reality is they are still controlled by Zoomanity.

I once had a visitor named Stuart.

Had he escaped from Zoomanity?

Stuart arrived (I was staying in his mother's home) and after light, smiling introductions he asked what I was eating for dinner that evening. I told him I had no idea as I had decided on this trip to do no cooking so would drive downtown to get some food.

He smiled and as he left he told me to hang around for him to return. I did. Where I am writing in the wild mountains of Bonny Doon in California there are wild rabbit, pig, deer, mountain lion, plenty of birds and wild food growing.

About an hour later he came back with a captured rabbit and freshly pulled and picked vegetables.

He asked me if I liked rabbit and that it was fresh. I asked how fresh. He replied that fifteen minutes ago the rabbit was running around the fields!

I said sure, I would love some. He then placed the rabbit on the kitchen work surface and began to go back into the garden where I was living and pull up all kinds of vegetables and herbs. He then returned to the kitchen. It was a joy to watch this guy make dinner with food direct from the ground and fresh from the wild fields.

We talked and he asked me if I would go shooting with him the following day. Yes I said I would love to. We did. That day we saw nothing to shoot but if we had it would have been to eat.

We both walked down to what is known locally as the big pasture halfway down the mountain. It's all long grass and was going dusk. Stuart sent me one way and told watch out for large wild pigs. He said if I see one I have two options: run like hell or shoot it.

Thankfully no options were required!

Stuart walked the other way. Just before dark we were to meet up at the point we left each other, and then we would walk back home, hopefully with fresh food for us and the neighbours (they all share the kill here).

It was getting pretty dark so I headed back up the hill to the big pasture where we had left each other. I got back before Stuart and he eventually arrived shoeless. By this point it was virtually pitch black.

Now the point we met wasn't exactly where we left each other; it was just a meeting point in the middle of a wild plain. Stuart then said, 'I have to find my shoes.' He had been hunting barefoot. I wore walking shoes and could feel every small stone beneath my feet. The mountain folk don't wear shoes most of the time. How these guys can do it is beyond me.

Stuart then put down his gun in the dark and walked in a different direction. In the middle of a vast long grass plain he went directly to his shoes and put them on. I was totally amazed. Was this an unused sense of the human I was seeing in action through another man? Had this man actually escaped from Zoomanity?

We sat down together, ate, drank and talked about how things are in downtown Santa Cruz. The very night before there had been two shootings and two deaths. The mountain people avoid the cities or the towns unless they have to go there.

They said to me (and there is a point to me telling you this story) that going into town disturbs them. It affects the way they think, the way the feel, and the way they are with life. They told me 'it's the vibe man' – the vibration and feel of the place that upsets them. Because of that they avoid going downtown.

I asked 'You must go for groceries?' He replied that now and then they go for staples and that is it. They told me there is no need for town when they have everything they need here.

I thought, here am I writing this book about escaping Zoomanity and I have been amongst people who have already done that.

Let me stress, these people are *not* fundamentalists in any way. They have cell phones, computers, iPods and more, but they live a self-reliant life. They are college graduates with good backgrounds yet they are opting for a life that is self-reliant and has broken away from Zoomanity.

I thought to myself later, if an animal escapes the zoo, most of the time at some point it grows weak and dies. It cannot cope not because its natural coping mechanisms have been removed or taken away, but they have been covered up by the zoo keepers over time to create passive reliant animals.

Isn't humanity the same in Zoomanity?

Think of it like this.

When you go into the city or town ?to do your grocery shopping, if you want meat you pay for meat and it is handed to you. If you want bread you pay for bread and it is handed to you. If you want drinks you pay for drinks and they are handed to you.

What if all of those systems were to collapse overnight? The systems put in place to give the zooman what the keepers feel you need to survive and stay passive?

Most of Zoomanity would have no idea how to go catch an animal and use it for food. Most of Zoomanity would have no idea how to grow wheat or grain and then make bread with it or even turn the grain into flour.

Zoomanity has taken away a natural liberty and made it easy for us. Why?

They make it easy. Just like the animals in the zoo, we become reliant on Zoomanity for our very survival.

They have become institutionalised. Haven't we? Could you go catch a rabbit right now then go find the right vegetables and herbs to make a dinner? Maybe you can – I am generalising – but the modern-day reality is most of mankind couldn't.

Look at history. When passive mankind has been left for whatever reason without the staples to survive it can end in rioting and even warfare or even worse – starvation and death.

Even in countries where people starve to death it's often not for lack of food. It's usually about control. Zoomanity will always want to control the human and create the zooman.

In Third World countries and even in the West, it's really no different; it's simply dressed in different clothes.

But the zoo animals can be rehabilitated. They can be taught to hunt and survive. The instinct was never removed, it was simply covered up.

Your real human instincts for discovery and excitement have never vanished. Yes, life might feel dull and like an endless trudge through knee-high mud, yet you can learn, you can discover, and you can rehabilitate yourself and become human again.

Think of a Russian doll. Remove each layer by layer until you get to the middle. Each layer is a thin veneer but the centre is a solid piece. This is like the zooman. He is layered in veneer after veneer but each veneer can be removed and peeled away until the human is released again. All you need to do to start this is simply wake up.

There is so much out there for us already, like Stuart who could find his shoes in the middle of nowhere in the pitch black. We have to uncover and rediscover, find our natural intuition, and allow ourselves to *feel* life again.

In an interesting twist, the rabbit-hunting guy was also hiding out from a failed relationship. He had been living in the wilderness for some time not wanting to return to his home place for fear of bumping into his ex.

Interesting, don't you think? A guy that appears to have left the trappings of Zoomanity behind, yet still the failings of Zoomanity to teach relationships may have resulted in the breakdown of his relationship and the subsequent avoidance tactic so as not to confront her after two years.

Zoomanity has so many controls that ultimately the human inside has to overcome the zooman on the surface to grow and thrive.

Ancient Humans Outside Zoomanity

This reminds me of a time I spent in the Ecuadorian jungles meeting the Achuar Indians after I did the fund raiser I mentioned earlier.

Not only do they live off the land, most have never seen a white man before and have never been outside their village community.

The villages consists of up to fifty people. The community is very close and tight knit but what really surprised me was how tuned into the earth, humanity and nature they are.

They are a dream-based culture which means they are so tuned into the natural intuition they base their thoughts and intentions around what takes place during their dreams.

Now if this sounds a little far out or over the top for you I strongly suggest you read a book called *Premonitions* published by Hay House to find out more on this subject.

Back to the Indians. I was offered the opportunity to go on a midnight walk with some of the Indians through the Amazon jungle. This walk took place in the middle of five million square acres of pure amazing jungle that most of mankind has not only never been to but barely knows exists.

So a group of us went out walking. The Indians took the lead. They find, hear, and see everything, even in the pitch black. They feel their way through.

They know the plant to take for a common cold. The plant for headaches, the plant to clear a chest that is sore, and more. They even picked up a small red upturned mushroom and told us that if a man suffers from deafness he had to hold the mushroom next to his ear, then crush the mushroom between his fingers. I tried it. When crushed a high frequency noise is heard and has a clearing effect in your ears. I have no idea if it works, how it works or why it works if it does. I'm just sharing a small story.

They can see animals without seeing them. They *feel* the presence of the animal. They know when danger is close – they feel it. They know when there are changes in the environment. They feel it.

They can feel and hear animals without the animals making a sound. I saw them spot a sloth at the top of a tree in a thick jungle despite the fact I could only see the animal with powerful binoculars.

There was more of course and maybe that's the subject for another book.

The real question is how do they do this and how come western man appears unable to do the same things?

The reality for the human – now the zooman – appears to be this: the Achuar are unconditioned. They are still like the wild animals outside the zoo. To eat they have to find and cultivate their own food. What's interesting is that they truly understand the ground, the seasons, the soils, and almost every aspect of horticulture. They understand yet they have never been to college or school.

The zooman is fed replacement foods, mixed with chemicals and cancer-creating extras to make foods last for months without decomposing.

Recently I moved home. On the top shelf was a box of cornflakes. I noticed they had been there over eighteen months. I also noticed they had not decomposed. Do you ever ask why? Food is designed to rot and go back to where it came from – the ground – yet we rarely ask why it stays apparently fresh and crisp for over eighteen months.

Just another thought. The way the Indians eat foods I found deeply interesting. They do not have fixed meals daily like breakfast, lunch, dinner, and snacks. They eat what they catch. If they do not catch food, they simply don't eat but drink a daily staple that is chewed from the root of a tree then spat out into a wooden bowl for everyone and anyone to drink as a carbohydrate at any point in the day.

Yes, I, like all visitors, had to accept the custom of the drink of manioc as you enter the village. Sounds disgusting drinking the spit of the Indians but it's truly another life experience.

The Indian schools are the schools of life, about life and creating life. Knowledge is passed on from the village elders about ancestors, survival, and enjoyment. They also of course tap into an unseen force that is relied upon for their daily life. What can I say – I saw it in action, it works, and is hard to deny!

As for modern schools – would you agree that most of what you, I, and our kids learn at school is an absolute total waste of time? It's almost a self-feeding system that educates kids to take in more information that has no real, true life value.

I sit and wonder if we were taught about money, relationships or faiths, wouldn't we be more informed people? Yet the zoo keepers want you to question nothing.

Schooling (which of course has its good points) is one of the main tools of Zoomanity for the conditioning of mankind. Get them young and condition them early. This way control is easier.

It cannot remove the human but it conditions, masks and covers it well enough so the zooman becomes reliant on a system designed to control and make the human being totally passive.

It's interesting that the mountain people here in California and the Indians in the jungle are all home schooled. I think the reasons, as this book explains, are clear.

While so-called educated nations continue to blow up, destroy each other and engage in war, there are people out there right now who are clearly escaping from Zoomanity and reaching back into humanity for solutions.

Fall of Zoomanity, Rise of Humanity

Is Zoomanity dead?

I believe at some point a massive switchover will take place.

Look at the way the monetary system works, based around greed and lust for more. It's unsustainable – the math shows that (as does common sense). The new leaders and the new lights of mankind are here already. They are not who you think they are. They are escapees and have already made their escape from Zoomanity. I predict change and a mass escape from Zoomanity. The human will return. He/she is here right now.

Can we continue going to war and inflicting on others our beliefs on what is the best way of life?

Can we sit back while families get lost and overdrawn into the complexity and destructive behaviour of mass consumption?

Can we allow the monetary system to carry on making a mockery of mankind, allowing the free control it has and being a rewarder of those who take the lead within its core?

Can we just sit around and watch as the media of Zoomanity and its chariots of endless lies and hype continue to train, condition and repeat endless, meaningless, selfish directions to mankind?

Of course, as always, there is more. I'll put that into another book maybe.

It's clear that change is needed and the day of the zooman is ending.

Here's the interesting stuff.

As these days come and go it's as if we have almost been in a trance, working robotically and doing what we should be doing or are told what to do.

Zoomanity is in control of you. You rarely question anything if at all. Think about it. The feeding starts when we are born and ends when we are dead. It begins each day when your eyes open and only ends when your eyes are closed.

A day becomes a week.

A week becomes a month.

A month becomes a year.

Years become our life.

We started work at sixteen and suddenly we are fifty years old and still working hard. Where did your time go?

But your life is time.

Who is in control of your time? Your life is time, tick-tocking away.

The food we digest on a daily basis appears to create almost hypnotic clones.

Here's another good example of how mind manipulation of the masses takes place at a very subtle level. Have you been affected by the following?

If you go to any newsstand on a Saturday or Sunday morning, you will see line after line of people walk in and walk out holding a newspaper.

Million upon millions are sold.

Now they all go home and read the same printed messages. What are the messages? Are they up building or depressing? Good or bad news?

Recently here at home I went around to my parents' house. They watch everything and have a TV in almost every room.

My mum said to me, 'What do you think about the guy in the Lake District?' (It's a place in England.)

I replied, 'What do you mean?'

She looked at me as if I had just landed from another planet. She said, 'It's been going on for days. You must have seen it.'

I replied that I had no idea what she was on about.

Mum then called dad and then said to him, 'Can you believe Alan has no idea what is going on in the Lake District?'

Dad looked at me as if I had just landed from Venus, said nothing, and just looked away at the TV. Then he asked mum if they had caught him.

The story was about a man on the rampage with a gun. A small story in a small part of the world. It would never affect your life in a million years, yet it was a story that had the nation hooked for days as if it were taking place in everyone's own neighborhood.

Zoomanity had sucked in the consciousness of a nation for a few days and held them in a place they didn't need to be.

Be honest – has that happened to you? It's happened to me. I can vividly recall switching on the TV the morning that Princess Diana was killed. The whole nation appeared to almost shut down.

And how about 9/11? You get the point. Again the nation was held tight in the grip of Zoomanity for what felt like forever. We see this more and more. Even as I edit this book we are in the thick of a Libyan battle that is 'new' news daily.

Who will win, why are we fighting, what happens next? Can you see what is taking place? The battle and the food you are fed is nothing more than a battle for your mind.

People talk about 'I can't wait until Friday' or tomorrow or some holiday. 'I can't wait' – then we spend all of our time looking forward until Saturday. Then we dread Sunday evening as we have to go back to work in the morning.

Who exactly says this is normal?

Why is it normal?

Do you want it to be normal?

Question it. Think about it.

If you are always looking forward to the weekend, what does that say about the other five days?

Do you not want to go to work, work hard, be under a controlling boss and be under the control of another person?

So if we do this all of our working life – let's say fifty years – that means 13,000 days of our working life we don't like. Isn't that sickening to see in black and white? For 13,000 days of our life we want them to end. Is that what you want? Who is it that says it has to be this way?

Think about what we are fed constantly by the media of Zoomanity. Zoomanity tells us to work hard. The rewards come at the weekends, the holidays we are allowed to go on once a year, or the bank holidays we are given as a gift of kindness from Zoomanity, much like when we give a pet dog a small treat.

These messages are continually fed to us through the mass messaging of Zoomanity.

Stand Back and Look

So let's take a step back here and look at ourselves. What do we bring into our mind and our senses on a daily basis?

Remember the list above. What do you allow into your daily space and allow to penetrate your mind? Of course you have had those moments when you read or hear something at the start of a day and you cannot shift it. Most of the time that is by pure chance. How about when it's done on purpose? Messages are fed to you to keep you docile so you will stay in line and do as you are told.

You see this is where Zoomanity is silently clever. They give us what they think we need to survive or what we want but the reality is what we *need* and what we *want* are two totally different things.

So the question is, how to we stop ingesting and digesting this barrage from Zoomanity? The reality is we cannot totally unless we go to the moon or go live in a cave. Yet we can take action to reduce our intake dramatically.

It might help if I share what I have done. Over the years. Myself.

In 2007 I got rid of TV as an information medium for myself. Does that mean I no longer watch TV? No, it doesn't; it means I control almost everything I watch. After a long self-imposed fasting from TV I decided to buy another. That feels more balanced. I rarely watch the news or the bad news that is on daily. Why would or should I? Let's think about this. How often does the news actually apply to us?

I laugh when I think about soap operas. In England we have *Coronation Street* and *East Enders* and quite a few more.

I can remember, especially when I was a hairdresser, conversations that would last for hours. People would talk about the lives of the people in the soap. They would say things like, 'What do you think she should do?' 'Do you think he should leave?' 'I think she'll find out?'

And then of course it would be a case of 'I can't wait until Wednesday to see what she does!'

Yet these are *not* real lives, they are fake representations of reality itself, representative of Zoomanity.

This is an educational process where our standards can be set from actors on TV, yet the fact is they are all the figment of the imagination of a script writer and the TV people.

Don't believe that's possible? Just go to Google and research 'what TV does to the mind.' I think you'll be shocked at the *real* effect of TV on the mind of a human.

I can be apathetic but don't need to be self-engrossed into something that really has no affect on my life.

These days we are bombarded with stories about the rich and famous and the next crisis they are facing or other disasters.

Let's be honest. Does the life of a football player, an actress or a wanna-be superstar with zero credentials really have to come into the influence of your life? If we allow that mind-garbage in, what effect does it have on us, on you? It creates a dump of some kind. Some will say if we don't watch the news we cannot know what is going on the world today. That's simply not true and this is where we have to exercise our natural inquisitive nature.

If I do watch the tube I watch movies or I will watch something I have specifically chosen to watch. I never allow the TV to run over. At the end of the show I simply switch off.

And here's another question. Does the remote control you, or do you control the remote?

You know how Zoomanity likes it to be. Take control.

The same goes for any other mainstream media. Radio? Unless it's music that switches you on and ignites you, switch it off. Newspapers? Can you truly say they are filled with good news? Don't give your cash away on them, read something that will challenge and inform you – if that's what you want, of course. Let's be really honest here: can you trust what you read in a mainstream newspaper? Yes, the story might be true but the slant or angle might have been twisted (as has often been proved with court cases).

But let's not lose the point here.

I'm certainly not saying they are bad things. I am saying we need to be aware of these endless distractions that can take any good conversation and dumb it down to almost meaningless nothing.

This is about the endless noise that enters into your mind, your thoughts, and your head, and creates a mass of noise thought that makes it almost impossible for any human to stay human. The result is the zooman living and in the tight grip of Zoomanity.

Can you make informed decisions and informed choices or is the noise so much that you simply get swept along in the flow of life?

You know the answer, of course, and when you do know the answer you are in a position to make changes.

Zoomanity understands control. They have been doing it since the birth of humanity followed by the creation of Zoomanity.

Are you wakening up? Are you seeing what is going on? How do you feel about your life so far? Have you had enough? Do you need change?

Zoomanity might have had you in its grip but now you are feeling and questioning things for yourself. This is an exciting time for you! Embrace it!

Are you or have you been under the spell of others for years, doing as you are told and staying in line for fear of disapproval? You do something, they tell you no. You say something, they tell you no. You want to do something, they again tell you no.

You've had enough. Things must change and change fast. Otherwise you'll wither and die inside.

Is it your job? You wife? Your husband? Your faith? Is it all of them and more? You've come this far in life and you have begun to realise that is just isn't what you expected, nothing like you were told.

It's time.

It's your time.

Your Escape from Zoomanity

All it takes is a second – a minute – a moment of your time. You'll barely notice it yet you'll know it's happened after it has happened.

The signs are clear.

Sudden discontent based on knowing that you've been unhappy for a long time. This time it's different, very different. This time you really have had enough.

Zoomanity no longer works for you and now there will be no stopping the change.

Let me illustrate.

For seventeen years I had my hairdressing salons. I had worked hard to make them work, make cash, keep clients, and keep on building and growing my business.

We had the number one position in the town.

The stuff I had to deal with on a daily basis included staff leaving, clients complaining, clients wanting more and more freebies, tax issues,

149

landlord issues, and all the other issues that go with running any mainstream business.

Once when I fired a member of staff, her mother rang threatening all kinds of actions. Unfortunately they knew where I lived. I was home and they came hammering at my front door. I of course pretended I wasn't home, and I hid behind the sofa whilst her crazy mother shared abuse via my open mailbox in my door.

Or the other time when I caught a member of staff stealing. I fired her. The next thing within thirty minutes her boyfriend raced into the salon and tried to kick down my office door whilst shouting how he wanted to break a few bones in my body! I of course in true hairdresser fashion hid under my desk hoping my flimsy fire-door wouldn't give way to his huge kicks. I survived!

Or even the time I got so behind on my taxes eventually the taxmen and bailiffs entered into my salon. The salon was absolutely packed with clients. They walked in, stood next to me as I cut a client's hair and simply said pay today or we will remove the salon furniture.

Pressure – but big lessons.

Other things I always found hard were when I had invested seven years into a member of staff only, for them to ask to see me at the end of the day on Saturday. I always knew what was coming. Five o'clock would arrive, and they would walk into my office and hand me their resignation. After seven years they would offer just a week's notice. When I asked where they were going they always lied and said they had no idea or a long way away or leaving the industry.

By the same time the following week, 99% of the time that same person that my salon had nurtured for seven years was working in another salon, sometimes just a few hundred yards from my salon.

That always hurt.

One day my manager did just this. I had seen this take place year after year for seventeen years. It was nothing unusual but this time I'd had enough.

I decided to sell my salon.

Can you relate to that moment? Change is needed urgently. Do we go for it or ignore it? This is the moment of shift in your inner being.

It can be a moment in a job, a moment in a relationship, a moment the way your life is right now.

Are you struggling with a dead end, mindless job that removes every ounce of your creative force? It gives you cash but removes your happiness? It feels hard everyday and gets nothing but harder and harder.

Are you in a relationship where the pain, the stress, the misalignment, the falling out, the bad words, the dullness or the silence is just getting too much for you now?

Laughing has been replaced by silence as the TV channel gets changed almost every thirty minutes in between a glass of wine or more hot drinks.

Have you had the moment?

The moment where you sit there and say to yourself, 'I have had enough!'

Zoomanity is telling you that change is wrong. Zoomanity tells you that change is bad, it won't work, you won't get a new job, you won't get a new relationship. Zoomanity controls you through your own fears.

No job means no life, right? No relationship means a lonely life, right?

Yet your moment has arrived or is racing faster and faster and faster towards your breaking point, your snapping, or the moment when tolerance has vanished forever.

It's not that you haven't tried. It's just that you now know for sure that if you stay in this place your soul will turn to dust and everything that makes you smile will vanish forever – or that's how it feels right now.

Another job will come. Another relationship will come. They always do. We just have to overcome the fears placed on us by Zoomanity.

When my moment arrived I knew I could no longer carry on with the salons. Everyone thought it was a crazy thing for me to do – to leave a career that I had been doing from the age of twenty to forty.

They told me I would never get another job. I could never become a writer. I knew better.

Has your moment arrived?

The Stop to Start

So you have had your moment.

Zoomanity and its curse will be playing with your inner thinking. You know what you want to do and where you want to go but almost everything will be telling you to stay where you are and don't change.

Remember that Zoomanity loves to control. It controls you through your fears. Zoomanity is the provider. Break the rules and they withdraw their support.

Remember *The Truman Show* at the start of this book. Fear-based control. Now you are facing your own fears. You know a change is needed and needs to come fast. If you make a change what will be the consequence of change?

This is your stop moment.

It's the moment where you must think and be as clear as you have to be.

How do you stop when Zoomanity is pushing your life so fast? The noise, the advice from everywhere and anywhere. How do you get clear?

You steal time back, then take time and take real time to think. That means unplugging and removing yourself from the noise of mankind.

What are you thinking about? Does it feel right? Does it feel wrong? Are you just being moody and miserable? Are you just having a moment? Is this something that has gone on for years and years and you really have hit your defining moment?

Back in the jungle when I spent time with the Achuar tribe in Ecuador I discovered something I have never seen before.

It wasn't meditation but it was something like this.

Meditation comes from mediating. So this is a process where you mediate with yourself and no one else.

The Indians in the jungle showed me how they closely knew themselves. They took time to think, to be alone, and to digest what is around them.

For example, on a walk through the jungle they would rarely say anything at all. They were so silent but they were fully awake. Awake to what? Awake to what was around them at every twist and turn.

When taking decisions they would go away and spend time alone in the jungle to be surrounded by nothing but real life. Real life as in trees, animals, and anything else you can think of.

This would be their stop moment so they could re-gather and think.

When I was in the Amazon one day we went to see the shaman. This involved a four-hour jungle trek and a one-hour river ride.

We got off the dug outs, jumped onto a mud bank around eighteen inches deep, and then had to hack our way into virgin jungle and follow the Indians as they took us to the village. This was to be a four-hour walk.

When we were just thirty minutes away from the tribe we all had to stop. We were told to stop and take a moment. This was common thing for them to do before entering the village.

We all had to part, take some banana plant leaves to quiet part of the jungle and think about what we were doing there.

I enjoyed twenty minutes of sheer reflection, although I had the fear of being eaten alive at any point from a large jaguar somehow sneaking up on me thinking I would taste better than monkey for once!

If they who lived in such isolation found the need to unplug, how more does it apply to a busy noisy zooman society to unplug?

How about you? When do you really stop? Where will you go to stop? How will you stop to take time to think and reflect your life?

Zoomanity is a never-ending stream of doing and doing more. The noise never ends. You are not supposed to think for yourself yet the reason you need to stop is so you can dig deeply into yourself and think.

Is this important? You bet. Every bad decision I have made in my life was a decision I made with no clear thought before, during or after.

Stop and think, has your moment arrived?

Now You Decide if You Are Ready To Escape!

Decisions, decisions, decisions. Life's full of them, don't you think?

Yet right now you are being shaped and defined by a moment when you awoke to the real situation your life is in right now.

You can feel it strongly – you know a decision must be taken. Problem is, there are generally two directions to go. The right way and the wrong way.

Now you can feel the power of stopping, but how do you know what is right?

When I stopped being a minister I knew it was the right thing for me personally. That doesn't mean my faith was wrong; I just felt it no longer served me the way I needed.

I had my moment and my thought but more importantly I had a feeling inside that was communicating to me how unhappy being the minister was for me. I knew that despite how hard it would be, a change had to be made.

The feeling inside was almost overwhelming. I ignored it and it got worse. I felt torn, ripped in two, and almost sick to the pit of my stomach knowing what I wanted to do but being unable to build the courage to do just that.

Zoomanity loves grey areas. Areas where we are confused and cannot decide. Zoomanity wants you to be held in a place where fear will override everything. And sometimes it really is black and white, not grey. If it no longer works it no longer works.

It works or it doesn't. If we want to fix it we can try, yet we know what is coming but can't act on what we know.

Why?

Fear of the consequences. Yet fear is an expectation of something that hasn't yet arrived. In other words the fear doesn't really exist!

Wherever you are, do you need to make a decision and make it fast?

Everyday we make decisions that affect other aspects of our lives. What should we eat, how should we dress, how do we look, and so on.

Today I am fitter than I have ever been in my forty-eight years. Four years ago I made a decision to start going to the gym on a regular basis. I dropped thirty-four pounds and reshaped.

Friends could believe how fit and healthy I began to look, yet their reactions were all the same. They all claimed they just didn't have time to go to the gym but their reality was they could make enough time each day to watch three or fours hours TV in the evening!

This was a decision that changed my life in a big way. Zoomanity doesn't like you to make a decision that will make a huge transformation in your life. It likes you to be a pack creature, and to accept and do as your told.

Do you have to make a decision that will affect the way you are forever – the way your life is forever? You want to know what to decide? You ask friends and you say, 'What will you do?' yet deep down you know what you should be doing. It's just if it goes wrong you can always blame them, right?

It's always your choice?

The Voice Inside

Do it, don't do it, go on do it, no don't do it.

Do you ever have that small voice repeating itself inside of you?

Some will say we are what we see and nothing else. I don't accept that.

Can you see the wind?

No, but you accept the wind is there of course, and there are lots of things in life we cannot see but we accept are there.

Inside of you there is a part of you that knows. It's in all of us – you, me, even the man next door.

What is it?

Have you ever walked into a room where you can feel the atmosphere is what people say 'thick' or 'heavy'?

Or have you met a person you don't like in an instant but you're not sure why? You can simply feel it?

Last year I had a visit to a friends place in California. He runs an organisation known as HeartMath (www.HeartMath.com). They showed me scientific data that shows how the energy field of all people creates an invisible boundary around the human body. In fact, they even proved this energy stands out from your body at a distance of around five feet away from the human body. Within that energy field your body sends out an invisible signal of a higher or lower frequency. When you feel a bad feeling about another person without knowing why, generally is it because they are giving off a lower vibration field than your own.

Go check out the HeartMath website for more mind-blowing proof, especially the information on 9/11.

Yet what is really interesting is that this voice is a voice that generally we ignore. When we feel things are not quite right it seems most of the time we just hope it will go away. Zoomanity likes it that way. It likes us to feel confusion and loss when a decision is to be made. It likes us to make no choice and listen to nothing apart from what we know.

Yet what do we know? We usually know what Zoomanity feeds us. These days we are having more and more of a real numbing of society on a daily basis. This almost kills the ability for us to feel and follow and dig deep into our inner voice, subconscious, inner being at a deeper level.

Are you listening? Are you hearing your voice? Can you feel what is right for you? Will you take action for you rather than for others? Will you do the right thing? Can you feel almost daily your voice saying to you, 'It's not this way at all'?

A good friend of mine said to me after her divorce, 'I always knew it wasn't right.'

I know you can hear it but will you listen?

The Law of Zoomanity or the Law of Humanity?

Are you a human being? Of course you are and as a human being you will have thoughts and feelings like everyone else.

I know a man. His name I can't say, just in case he reads this book (he asked me if he should read it, I told him yes, of course). Every time he is asked to make a decision on anything he always says things like, 'I'll see what she thinks', 'What do you think?' or 'Who can I ask?'

He also moans about the state of his life and how it never changes. He tells everyone how his wife is horrible to him. He also moans about how bad his job is, how he'd love his own business and how he is looking forward to retiring.

He is the ultimate zooman being – the perfect form and display of what a zooman should be.

He questions nothing.

He does as he is told.

He is very average.

His life is always the same.

He never has adventure.

Never has passion.

He barely looks alive.

You know why?

Ask him and he always say, 'I just get on with it.'

Really, is that how we were created? Like the zoo animals whose wild nature was replaced by the showmen?

Were humans created to live and experience life? Were you created or made that way? Do you want to be able to create the experiences you really want and truly need to make you feel alive almost daily?

If you've read this far you are wakening up from the restrictions of Zoomanity. You are becoming conscious of your own spiritual requirements as a human being. The life of Zoomanity has proved itself in your life to be a failure. You no longer have a desire to wait until you're sixty-five and retiring. You want more freedom for your spirit *right now*. Let's be frank: some day you, like all of us, will die. Are you getting what you want out of your life on earth or is Zoomanity telling you how it should be?

The Law of Humanity is greater than the Law of Zoomanity. Zoomanity can never be stronger yet its hold appears greater for the reason that it rules through fear. Facing your fears beyond your moment will give you ultimate power of the control of Zoomanity and then your natural law of humanity will become the over-riding force in your life.

Even then at some point you will have to face other laws. I personally had to face the Law of Deconstruction, where my life was absolutely left deconstructed and construction had to take place from the ground up.

We see this with buildings.

It is a pretty common thing for buildings to be totally flattened rather than being patched up. You can of course patch up an old building but it's still an old building with patches.

Life's like that sometimes.

My own parents could have struggled to keep patching up their own lives amongst the culture of poverty they started married life in with their young children, but they decided to deconstruct their early lives and allowed a construction of a new life to take place.

Don't underestimate what is taking place inside you right now as you read this book. Bigger, invisible laws are working their way among you and among us all.

You as a human being always know best but you rarely *know* you know best.

An old man sat by me and in his hand was a Russian doll. He asked me to remove the top layer and tell him what I could see?

I told him a shell.

He asked me to remove the next layer and asked me what I could see?

I told him another empty shell.

He asked me to remove a third layer and again asked me what I could see?

I told him again I could see a hollow, thin shell.

I removed five more shells until I got to the last one.

Now he asked me a final time: What do you see?

I said to him a solid doll.

He replied, 'This is life itself.'

We are covered by layers like the Russian doll. Each layer that covers is simply another veneer to replace the last one. Finally there are so many veneers we can forget what is in the middle. Yet the truth is also that each layer, each veneer, each cover can be removed until finally we return to the solid piece of the tree or the true essence of man.

This is you.

The veneers are the instructions, the rules, the prisons, the boxes, the doors, the restrictions of Zoomanity. You can masterfully remove each one at a time and recover, rediscover, reveal, and release your own humanity. And when you do – when you have finally done that – you are living a life like never before.

You wake each day and smile. You are excited about everything, everyone, every aspect of your life. You use each hour, each day as another experience. You see, feel and experience your life with amazement.

Then and only then can you say to yourself, YES!

I escaped!

I escaped from Zoomanity.

Manifesto

You have one life.

Know it or not … Your life is encased in your Zoomanity.

Zoomanity says question nothing.

I say question everything.

Zoomanity says stay in line.

I say step off the line and walk your own way.

Zoomanity wants to control you.

I say you control you

Free spirits, lovers of life, you were not born to live, not born to exist, you were born to be alive.

To be alive you need to express, you must create, you have to feel and listen to what your 'being' is saying to you, your humanity.

You also must resist. Resist the repeaters, the conditioners, the Zooman shapers, their controlling teachings, they, the zoo keepers, their life cages, the very constructs that Zoomanity has placed around you and your life.

Your potential, yes you do have potential, potential to live, to react, to create, to embrace the day, your day, each and every day with a smile of life, a thought of life another day for you to truly be alive.

Zoomanity says no, you must stay in their boundaries.

Zoomanity says no, you must do as your told.

Zoomanity says, fear, live in your fears.

Zoomanity says repeat and do, repeat and do, repeat and do.

I say no, I say run, I say feel, I say be in the place you feel your best, feel, yes feel your very best. Encourage your baby genius, feed your pulsating heart, tease, love and stroke your very soul, the same soul that thrives, cries, screams for freedom, release and joy.

Zoomanity says live life in the cage, stay in the cage, never leave the cage.

Humanity says your life is to be lived in the freedom of the earth, where nature calls you to BE, live, enjoy your experience, the experience of life itself.

Zoomanity says you, you are not great, you cannot do, you must not try, you must hold back.

Your life is to be loved, encouraged and guided to great things, greater, magnificent things, things of wonder, moments of awe.

You were created and gifted with a life superior to the Zooman. The Zooman, a manufactured, controlled drone of Zoomanity with its Zoomanic rules, restrictions and endless heartless conditioning. A life built around future dreams, future hopes and days that never arrive.

Live a life fulfilled now, embrace a vision of you, embrace a life that takes you out of Zoomanity, a life that is lived, loved and adored.

Now is the time for all of mankind to embrace an older, uncovered, rediscovered, newer paradigm of change, now is the time for you to rise, release the human within, take control of your life and live life on the terms of your human, the terms that you were gifted at birth.

The end of Zoomanity is near, the birth of a new humanity is upon us. Not driven by the dreams of wealth, not driven by dreams of more, not driven by dreams of the consumer-zoomerism and the thoughts of greed, lust, more, more, more.

This is the dream of being you, complete, be in, BE-IN there right now. Where your moment is fulfilled, happy, satisfied and clear.

Can you agree, should you agree, will you agree?

I have but one life.

My life is my time, time is my life. I promise to use my life to the fullest extent possible, in harmony with a greater good for others, wherever and whenever I can. Zoomanity has no hold on me.

I have consciously made a decision not to allow my Zoomanity and it's fools to make decisions for me, this way when things go wrong I will accept them, learn from them, discover from them and rejoice in them.

I have made a decision that I am a creative human being and will no longer accept the restraints of Zoomanity. I am and shall be the free spirit with godly abilities that should always be expressed even when Zoomanity say no, I will express my feelings, thoughts and ideas with the freedom of a human being.

I reject Zoomanitys confining rules and will embrace and live my true human nature, that same nature that is crying to be released and will be let loose for a better, happier stronger, fulfilled life. When the masses walk one way, I am committed to walking the other.

I declare myself a human being, self reliant on my feelings, my inner thoughts and natural laws of creation, a man to be seen as a revolutionist, dissident, a man of the present no longer held by Zoomanity – free from the restraints of Zoomanity.

I have escaped, I am free, I have escaped from my own Zoomanity.

How about you?

About The Author

Alan Forrest Smith is a writer, poet, modern day philosopher, iconoclast, artist, father and master of words.

Despite being his first book, Alan has been using words in a masterful way in business for himself and been hired by some very well, highly acclaimed business persons to write creative, persuasive words in print.

Escape from Zoomanity Vol I is his first book. Escape from Zoomanity Vol II, The Great Escape will be available very soon.

As you can imagine, Alan is also an acclaimed, highly motivational, truly inspiring public speaker. He has spoken in places such as New Zealand, Australia, USA, Malaysia, Singapore, former Soviet union country Latvia, England, Ireland and of course his beloved Scotland.

Alan Forrest Smith

www.AlanForrestSmith.com
www.EscapefromZoomanity.com
www.ZoomanityNation.com
www.fivelawsofescape.com

What's Next

From

Alan Forrest Smith

FREECommunityWebsite

www.ZoomanityNation.com

Zoomanity Nation is a FREE resource where you can log in, share your views, share your thoughts and be part of a nation of real-life escapees or potential escapees from Zoomanity.

It's designed to be a nation working, planning and talking together. It's your to access free.

Simply go to the website, register absolutely free and enjoy this free resource from Alan.

New Book

www.EscapefromZoomanity.com

NEW BOOK COMING 2012,

Escape from Zoomanity, Volume II

The Great Escape

The follow up to Escape from Zoomanity is your action plan to Escape from Zoomanity.

You'll discover how to

- Return to your real human being
- Recover and live your dreams
- Understand your over-whelming feelings of escaping from Zoomanity
- The daily pressure that keep you enslaved and how to break free
- Creating a realistic view of escape from Zoomanity
- How to build a plan that is in tune with you
- Removing conditioning and repeatist beliefs
- Understanding the natural laws of the human
- And so much more.

General release is spring 2012.

Live Tour, Speaking Dates

Alan Forrest Smith
&
Escape from Zoomanity Live

If you'd love to hear, see and experience Alan live, be the first to get notified about live dates, great offers and more, go to Alan's main website and sign up for Alan's notification letter. We'll do the rest, keeping you up to date on live dates, new releases and more.

Main Website

www.AlanForrest Smith.com

BUY A SHARE OF THE FUTURE IN YOUR COMMUNITY

These certificates make great holiday, graduation and birthday gifts that can be personalized with the recipient's name. The cost of one S.H.A.R.E. or one square foot is $54.17. The personalized certificate is suitable for framing and will state the number of shares purchased and the amount of each share, as well as the recipient's name. The home that you participate in "building" will last for many years and will continue to grow in value.

Here is a sample SHARE certificate:

YES, I WOULD LIKE TO HELP!

I support the work that Habitat for Humanity does and I want to be part of the excitement! As a donor, I will receive periodic updates on your construction activities but, more importantly, I know my gift will help a family in our community realize the dream of homeownership. **I would like to SHARE in your efforts against substandard housing in my community!** *(Please print below)*

PLEASE SEND ME _____ SHARES at $54.17 EACH = $ $_____

In Honor Of: _____

Occasion: (Circle One) HOLIDAY   BIRTHDAY   ANNIVERSARY

OTHER: _____

Address of Recipient: _____

Gift From: _____ *Donor Address:* _____

Donor Email: _____

I AM ENCLOSING A CHECK FOR $ $_____ PAYABLE TO HABITAT FOR HUMANITY **OR** PLEASE CHARGE MY VISA OR MASTERCARD *(CIRCLE ONE)*

Card Number _____ Expiration Date: _____

Name as it appears on Credit Card _____ Charge Amount $ _____

Signature _____

Billing Address _____

Telephone # Day _____ Eve _____

PLEASE NOTE: Your contribution is tax-deductible to the fullest extent allowed by law.
Habitat for Humanity • P.O. Box 1443 • Newport News, VA 23601 • 757-596-5553
www.HelpHabitatforHumanity.org

CPSIA information can be obtained at www.ICGtesting.com
Printed in the USA
BVOW021332171111

276301BV00001B/1/P